LOOKING AT THE VILLAGE FROM INDIAN HILL

Hinckley Township
or
Grand Lake Stream
Plantation

A Sketch by
MINNIE ATKINSON

Printed by the
NEWBURYPORT HERALD PRESS
Newburyport, Massachusetts

Notice

In many older books, foxing (or discoloration) occurs and, in some instances, print lightens with wear and age. Reprinted books, such as this, often duplicate these flaws, notwithstanding efforts to reduce or eliminate them. The pages of this reprint have been digitally enhanced and, where possible, the flaws eliminated in order to provide clarity of content and a pleasant reading experience.

Hinckley Township or Grand Lake Stream Plantation [Maine]
Two Volumes in One

By:
Minnie Atkinson

Copyright © 1920, Minnie Atkinson

Originally published:
Newburyport, Massachusetts
1920

Reprinted by:

Janaway Publishing, Inc.
732 Kelsey Ct.
Santa Maria, California 93454
(805) 925-1038
www.JanawayGenealogy.com

2016

ISBN: 978-1-59641-378-8

Made in the United States of America

ACKNOWLEDGMENT AND FOREWORD

For the information contained in these pages thanks are due and gratefully given to Mr. and Mrs Arthur Wheaton, Mr. W. B. Hoar, Mr. Truman Brown, Mr. David Welch, Mr. W. G. Rose, Mrs. Thomas Calligan, Mr. and Mrs William Gollin, Mr. and Mrs James Sprague, Mrs Frank Holmes, Mr. Frederick Foster, Mr. John Story, Mr. Stephen Sprague, Mr. Stephen Yates, Mrs. Augustine Mc Donald, Mr Charles Calligan, Mrs. Jackson Brown, Mr. Abraham McArthur, Mrs. Alonzo Woodward, Mrs. Ellen Hawkins and many others of Grand Lake Stream, to Mrs Martha Gould of Township 27, to Louis Mitchel of Pleasant Point and to Joe Mitchel of Peter Dana's Point. Mr. Charles A Rolfe of Princeton has been especially kind in furnishing much valuable information in regard to the Princeton and Milford road, early sportsmen and other matters. Messrs. Joshua Crockett, William Robinson and Orington Brown, life long residents of Princeton and its vicinity, the first two with memories reaching back nearly eighty years, have given valuable information of lumbering, lumber firms and pioneers of Hinckley. Mr. John Gardner of Calais has furnished some interesting facts. To Mr. Wallace Brown of the latter city thanks are due for several Indian stories and the Indian mythology. Mr. James Vroom of St. Stephen has also contributed information. In addition to his report in various numbers of the "Report of the United States Fish Commissioner," from which extracts have been freely made, Mr. Charles G. Atkins of Bucksport has furnished data of the earliest fish cultural work in the village. Mr. C. J. Webber of Bangor has given valuable information from the records in his office and Miss Alice R. Farnum, first assistant in the Massachusetts Archives Department, has given aid in the search of old records. The Land Office in Augusta has been most courteous in answering many letters of inquiry.

Information has been gathered from many sources in

addition to those mentioned. It has often come from chance conversations and from desultory reading. It would be impossible to trace all its sources, but an earnest effort has been made to weave it all into a true story of Hinckley Township.

To the people of Grand Lake Stream who have patiently told me their unwritten annals I wish to say that my best hope of the history is that it will express somewhat of the deep regard I have for them, and perhaps in some measure repay their trouble in its behalf. I am conscious that it will fall short of expectations. Despite vigilance there will be almost certainly inaccuracies and omissions. It is with many misgivings that it is at length sent to the printer.

This remote Township may seem to the casual visitor like one of the spare ends of our country, too little developed to be important or interesting, too sparsely populated to need depicting. My manuscript has grown, nevertheless, breaking from the original thought of what it should be (the entertainment of a few idle weeks) and taking an unexpected shape, and length and much time in its preparation. The work has been extremely interesting.

Here, when white men first came, was a sort of inverted Nirvana where all was change yet nothing changed: years passed but brought no age; countless generations of trees, beasts, birds and fishes lived and died— all indistinguishable one from another. One year was every year. Winds, lightenings, rain and frost worked havoc but altered nothing. Life, prolific, strong and rapacious, gained nothing. Indians snatched a scanty sustenance from land and water but arrested none of the savage inertia, nor wrought changes in themselves. No living thing here sought variation, or looked backward or forward. Nature's goal was forgotten, abandoned or reached. Life, decay, litter, and again life, decay, litter unending, always the same.

From the time of the De Monts settlement in 1604 on an island near the mouth of the St. Croix river white men occasionally penetrated into these wilds. Trappers, hunters, explorers, adventurers, men from the fort of La Tour on the St. John river and from the Seigniory of the Baron de la Castine on the Penobscot river sometimes passed along these lakes and carries. A Jesuit priest in his sable robes may have brought a passing touch of deeper gloom. As the eighteenth century neared its end soldiers of the Revolution and then surveyors came here also. These were portends of events to come. They left no marks. Early in the nineteenth century lumbermen began to operate in the vicinity. Then a new force, human wills seeking a definite end, began the rout of savagery. A slow, uncertain but actual march of events began.

Thus was ushered here the courageous, picturesque, adventurous, hale human life that took root and thrived. The pioneers, the rude epic of the tannery, the play of sportsmen are all acts in a drama whose plot is the maintenance of life under difficulties. This history can do little to reveal the struggle, or the joy, sorrow and unconscious faith that has attended it, but perhaps the facts here set down will awaken the imagination of readers and thus be a medium to convey understanding of it.

Newburyport, Massachusetts.

CONTENTS

Mythology	Passamaquoddy Tribe
Chapter I	Location and some Early History
Chapter II	Under the Jurisdiction of Massachusetts, Logging
Chapter III	Squatters, Sportsmen, First Road
Chapter IV	The Tannery
Chapter V	The Village
Chapter VI	Lakenwild
Chapter VII	The Tannery Concluded
Chapter VIII	Hinckley Township becomes Grand Lake Stream Plantation
Chapter IX	Later Days in the Village
Chapter X	Grand Lake Stream in the World War
Chapter XI	Description of the Village
Chapter XII	Fish and Game
Chapter XIII	The Hatchery
Chapter XIV	Later Indians
Chapter XV	The Sewing Circle, The Church
Chapter XVI	Witteguergaugum
Appendix	Poems, Indian Names, Demons and Stories

ILLUSTRATIONS

Looking at the village from Indian Hill   Frontispiece

The Stream below Big Falls

The Saw Mill

The Dam

Grand Lake Hotel

The School House

Boynton's Camps

Treadwell's Camps

Ball's Camps

Fishing from a Pier

The Stream and Second Hatchery

The Church

Mythology of the Passamaquoddy Indians

In the beginning, used to say the Indians, Klooscup, the first man, formed all things. All the animals then were of the same size. The lively flea jumped forty miles. This was too rapid locomotion for the best interests of all concerned. So Klooscup rubbed him down until he became very little. The moose, on the other hand, was so stupid that he would neither do harm nor be unduly exuberant so he was rubbed larger. The squirrel ran up a tree so fiercely that he tore it down. He was rubbed smaller. Thus Klooscup rubbed everything larger or smaller according to the nature which it displayed. The trees were next formed, and the ash tree made king of them all. Klooscup stuck a great many bows and arrows into it, and presently out came men and women.

There was an old witch, called Poochinquis, who used to go up and down the forests crying; "I want your babies! I kill babies!" Klooscup caught her, cut her up in pieces, and threw the pieces into the water. Out of these pieces came the mosquitoes, the flies and all the bad insects, with the exception, of course, of the fleas.

Thus the world was made ready for the needs and story of human life.

HINCKLEY TOWNSHIP
or Grand Lake Stream Plantation
Chapter I
Location of Township and some of its Early History

Almost in the center of the old Passamaquoddy land lay a tangled chain of lakes and streams like trinkets of silver on the deep green of the earth. Largest of all the lakes was Witteguergaugum, now called Grand lake and next largest was Genesagenagum, renamed Big lake. Between these two and projecting broadly to the east and north was the wilderness that became Hinckley Township. Into Grand lake the water of thirty-two other lakes and ponds flows.* Three streams empty it into Big lake, thence through Long and Lewey lakes and by way of the St. Croix river the water flows to Passamaquoddy bay. The largest and middle of these streams is Grand lake stream. It has two water falls and is full of little rips. Nearly all of it is within the borders of Hinckley. It is three miles long, and runs almost diagonally across its southwestern corner. Bonney brook, the easterly stream of the three, is entirely therein. The third outlet, Little river, lies in the Township to the west which is Number 6, Range 1. The southern extremity and an eastern cove of Grand lake, and the northwestern part of Big lake are in Hinckley.

The chief settlement of the ancient Passamaquoddy tribe (once called Sabbayk and by the French classed with the Penobscot and Micmack Indians as Etchemins) was near the bay, but members of the tribe made frequent migrations

---

*The lakes and ponds flowing into Grand lake are Pocumpass, Warbash, Sistadobsis (Dobsis) Upper Sistadobsis, Junior, Scragley, Pleasant, Shaw, Horseshoe, Bottle, Keg, Norway, Pug (flowing into Junior bay of Grand lake) Pug (flowing in Dobsis) Duck, Mill Privilege, Pond, Lumbert, Lowell, Glaspy, Hasty Cove, Pickerel, Trout, McClellen Brook, Whitney Cove, 1st Ox Brook, 2nd Ox Brook, Dyer Cove, Killborn, 1st, 2nd and 3rd Chain lakes.

up into this region. Sometimes as many as twenty families would paddle up through the lakes, one family in a canoe, one canoe behind another—a long, silent, single line. When the travelers reached the head of Big lake—if they were going still further—they would carry the canoes, inverted over the heads and resting on the shoulders of the men, along the east bank of Grand lake stream to Grand lake. An Indian carry, so much used that even the rocks are worn, was thus made across the corner of the Township. Favorite camping places were upon the west bank of the stream near Grand lake and upon the lower eastern shores of the lake. In the former place many Indian relics have been found. Sometimes the Indians pushed to the head waters of Grand, or to the further lakes. In the Autumn and Winter these trips were hunting expeditions. When deer were sought the hunters, epuipped with snow shoes, skimmed over the snow easily in the chase, but the deer sank through the snow, were speedily exhausted and easily killed with clubs. Often wolves would come down from the northern forests, and drive away the deer for many seasons. At such times the tribe would suffer from hunger. The migrations in the spring, in later times, were often for the purpose of making sugar.

Sometimes Mohawks made incursions into the Passamaquoddy land and attacked these peaceful camping parties. At the head of Grand lake is a narrows which connects it with Pocumpass lake. It is called "The Thoroughfare." Fragments of a tradition tell of an attack by Mohawks upon a party of Passamaquoddies at this point. A number of Indian graves on the east shore are said to contain the bodies of warriors who fell in the battle. Many arrow heads and other weapons are still found about the spot.

The story of the battle runs thus:

When the terrifying cry of the Mohawks rang through the woods the surprised Passamaquoddies defended themselves desperately. So fierce was the ensuing onset that a brook, trickling into the lake in the midst of it, ran red and

LOCATION AND EARLY HISTORY 3

thus received a baptism of blood, and a christening for it has since been called Blood brook. With the coming of darkness the din and slaughter of battle halted. In the night the remaining remnants of Passamaquoddies fled in canoes down the lakes to a point on Big lake called Peter Dana's Point in honor of one of the more notable chiefs, or governors of the tribe. The Mohawks had no canoes. The fugitives hoped they could not follow. Nevertheless lookouts were stationed on high land and in the tops of trees. A day of anxiety wore on. Late in the afternoon there was a cry of alarm. Above the tops of the trees on the west side of Grand lake a flurry of dead leaves rose in an ominous and advancing cloud. The sign was easily read. The Mohawks were coming and so rapidly that the wind of their passage drove the leaves upward. The Passamaquoddies took to their canoes and disappeared from the spot, hurrying to one of the remote recesses of this remarkable and intricate system of lakes and streams where the Mohawks could not find them.*

Another and still more fragmentary tradition tells of the final combat in the warfare with Mohawks. This version of it was told some time ago by Nicholas Lola, a chief of the tribe, to one of his white friends. Indians of a former generation were fond of telling these traditions and would become very excited in the recital.

This fight began at Loon bay on the St. Croix river, and showed excellent generalship on the part of the Passamaquoddies—if the manoeuvre was not incited by some adventurous white man, probably a Frenchman. A few fighters were placed in advance of the main body of Indians. Their duty was to fall back and entice the Mohawks to follow them. The main body of Passamaquoddies also constantly fell back, the taunting savages in front of them drawing the Mohawks on.

"They go back and back," said Nicholas Lola. "They

*In an article entitled "The Abanaki Indians", Frederick Kidder attributes the historical obscurity of this tribe partly to the water ways of their territory which afforded many and safe hiding places. "Collections of Maine Historical Society", Vol. VI.

all go back to narrow part of Grand lake and there we fight!"

To stimulate the warriors to frantic enthusiasm just before the final battle the Medicine Man of the tribe dressed himself in a bear skin. Going a little in advance of the army he told them to shoot arrows at him. If he turned and came back to them it would be a sign that they would be defeated in the battle, but if he went toward the enemy they were to follow and they would win.

"That fellow," said Nicholas Lola, "he look just like a bear. We shoot arrows: he run forward and we lick 'em good!"

Although no dates are attached to these stories, if the events are historical, they probably occured more than two hundred and fifty years ago when Mohawks terrorized so many white settlers and Indian tribes in eastern Canada and northern New England.

After the discovery of America this north eastern part of the continent fell into the possession of the French. Jesuit Missions were established in eastern Maine, Nova Scotia and Canada, and the Indian owners of Hinckley soon became converts to the Catholic faith. When the English obtained possession of the strip of land between the Penobscot and St. Croix rivers, in the early part of the seventeenth century, it, like the rest of Maine, was annexed to the Massachusetts Bay Colony. The Indians here helped somewhat in the war made on settlers who early pushed as far east as the Kennebec river. They took an active part in the Revolutionary War on the American side. Washington was held in almost sacred esteem by them. He sent letters to each of three tribes of the vicinity— the Penobscot, the Passamaquoddy and the St. John—exorting them to faithfulness in the American cause. The Passamaquoddy tribe still treasures its letter.* Delegates of these three tribes went to Watertown to meet the Massachusetts Council. Through their spokesman, Ambrose St. Aubin, chief of the

*This letter is in possession of the Pleasant Point branch of the tribe.

LOCATION AND EARLY HISTORY 5

St. Johns, they promised to adhere to the American cause, but asked in return a favor.

*"We want," said St. Aubin, "a black gown, or French priest. Jesus we pray to: and we will not hear any prayers from Old England."

So carefully had Massachusetts put up barriers against Catholics that it was sometime before a priest was procured for them.

**Col. John Allan was "Superintendent of Indian affairs in the Eastern Department and Commander of the Port of Machias." The Indians were greatly attached to him. An account of their activities during this war belongs to the history of Machias, but it is pertinent to say that if they had not been zealous assistants in the defence of that place all of the territory east of the Penobscot river would have been lost to Maine. Notwithstanding the "artful guiles of the enemy" to win their help they did, with very few exceptions, remain faithful to the American cause.

The old Indian routes—one starting at the Passamaquoddy bay and following the western branch of the St. Croix river, the other starting from Machias and following the Machias river and short portage to Big lake—over these lakes and carries to the Passadumkeag river were the inland routes to the Penobscot river. They were constantly used during the war. Col. Allan sometimes sent his despatches this way and thus westward to Massachusetts. Once very important ones were captured on the Penobscot river by British agents. Col. Allan himself was nearly captured on one of these lakes. He was traveling on skates when "he was set upon by a party of Indians in the service of the British, also mounted on skates. They gave chase and closely pressed him for a mile or two, when coming to an open place, a channel of water, he gave a tremendous jump and landed safely on the other side."

*"Historical Magazine," July 1869.
**This information pertaining to Col. John Allan and the Indians is nearly all taken from a book compiled from the Journals and letters of Col Allan by Frederick Kidder, called: "Military Operations in Eastern Maine and Nova Scotia during the Revolution." Published 1867.

On a spot near the Grand lake stream carry there is a lonely grave where a soldier, possibly of this war, was buried. Whether he was American or British is not known.* From Eastport upward along the west bank of the Passamaquoddy bay are many graves of Indians who fell defending this eastern territory.

In 1793 Col. Allan writes in his report on the Indian tribes: "On the lakes you will find numbers of Indians from Canada, St. Johns, Penobscot and the Mickmack Country, pesuing their several employments agreeable to the seasons. Some constant residents, and many of them for years not seen on the sea coast, being perpetually on the move."

The Indian owners of Hinckley also took part in the War of 1812. There are traditions that some of the command of John Brewer, Brigadier General of Militia in Washington County, came up through the Township over the old carry.

A few years ago, near this carry, a copper coin was found which was dated 1776. On one side was a likeness of George the third, on the other an effigy of an Indian on a prancing horse. The Indian's right arm was upraised, and in his hand a long spear was poised. Near the feet of the horse was a coiled rattlesnake with its head uplifted. The coin was about the size of a Canadian penny, and had a hole in it. It had evidently lain in the ground a long time. It may have been dropped by a soldier of one of these two wars, or, it is surmised, it may have been struck as a medal for the Indians, and been dropped by one of them.

When in the last months of the War of 1812 the English troops held all the land east of the Penobscot river and administered the civil government from Bangor, the Indians did, for a short time, once more fall under the sway of the disliked England. England proposed to make of this conguest a separate province of the Canadian government, and to call it New Ireland. When the Peace of Ghent was signed, however, Hinckley and the rest of eastern Maine were once more saved to the United States.

*It was probably an Englishman buried here since an American would almost certainly have been carried to Machias for burial. See verses in the Appendix.

THE STREAM BELOW BIG FALLS

CHAPTER II
Under the Jurisdiction of Massachusetts and Logging

The Massachusetts Bay Colony seems to have given little attention to her lands beyond the Penobscot river. They were inhabited by hostile Indians and "renegade Frenchmen." Of the latter there were but few, and in an act, passed in 1721, to prohibit trade or commerce of any sort with the Indians the Bay Colony makes no mention of them. The following section of the act shows how determined she was to stamp out all intercourse. "That whoever shall, after the first day of October next, directly or indirectly have any trade or commerce by way of gift, barter or exchange, or any way whatsoever, with any of the aforesaid Indians, or shall supply them with any provisions, clothing, guns, powder, shot, bullets or any goods, wares or merchandise whatsoever shall forfeit and pay the sum of five hundred pounds, and suffer twelve months imprisonment without bail or main prize, upon the first conviction; the said forfeiture to be recovered by bill, plaint or information in any of his majesty's courts of record—one half to him, or them, who shall inform and sue for same." Upon a second conviction an offender against this law was to be "deemed a felon and suffer the pangs of death."

A few settlements were made in the interior of eastern Maine prior to the Revolutionary war, but there are no obtainable records to show whether or not there were any within the limits of the tract later to be called Hinckley. It seems as if somebody must have migrated into these forests very early for in the deed which Massachusetts later gave of the Township she makes provision for the rights of settlers who were here before 1784.

This Township, though near, was not included in the million acres of land set aside for lottery prizes by means of which, shortly after the Revolutionary war, Massachusetts undertook to raise revenue for her exhausted treasury.

When the lottery lands practically all passed to William Bingham of Philadelphia a rather curious thing happened. According to a paper found among those of Mr. John Gardner, for fifty years a surveyor in this region, the lottery land, as originally surveyed, fell a little short of the million acres. In order to give Mr. Bingham the full amount of his purchase an additional strip, two miles wide and thirty six miles long, was surveyed and conveyed to him. Such a strip is marked on a very old map preserved in the Massachusetts archives, but it stretches across the tops of six Townships west of Hinckley. They are in the same line, however, and doubtless when in 1794 Samuel Titcomb surveyed and marked off the Townships of Washington County he made those of Range One, in which Hinckley is Number Three, the unusual distance of eight miles from the northern to the southern limits in order to conform with this line. At all events the Townships of this range are eight miles in extent north and south and six miles east and west.

In the same year that Washington County was surveyed, and its gloomy forests marked by invisible lines into named tracts, Massachusetts made a treaty with the Indians. Township Two, just east of Hinckley, was set aside for them, and much other land in this vicinity. In Township Three one hundred acres of land on the end of a point that extends into Big lake, and also Pine island, the northern part of which is in the Township, were reserved for them. The point is, on some old records preserved in the State House in Boston, called Nemcass. It is now usually called Governor's point because several Indian chiefs, or, as they are now called, Governors, have resided there.

The treaty with the Indians established for them the "privilege of fishing on both branches of the River Schoodic" (the St. Croix river)" without Hinderance or Molestation, and the privilege of passing the said river over the different Carrying Places thereon."

The Commonwealth of Massachusetts was now ready to dispose of her Townships in this part of the District of Maine, and anxious to have them settled. Township Three,

Range One, was contracted for by Titus Goodman and Seth Wright in 1794. There seems to be no further record of Mr. Wright's connection with the contract. It was Titus Goodman who promised to pay the Commonwealth 2905 pounds, 18 shillings and 9 pence for these many acres of woodland. According to the crumbling "Report of the Commissioners for the Sale of Eastern Lands on June 16th, 1795," Goodman paid 207 pounds of this sum, and gave his note for 2698 pounds, 18 shillings and 9 pence. He was a son of Captain Noah Goodman, a political leader of South Hadley. Close by in Northampton lived Samuel Hinckley, a judge of the Probate Court and an owner of various townships, one of them being what is now Rochester, N. Y. When, either because of financial embarrassment, or for other reasons, Goodman did not pay this note Judge Hinckley as his assignee, paid into the treasury of the Commonwealth the money due on the purchase, by that time computed in dollars and cents, and became the proprietor of the Township. If the amount of Goodman's note equalled the $9019.80 which Judge Hinckley paid then a pound in those days must have equalled in our money about $3.34. Thus the price originally paid for the Township approximated $9711.18. It became known as Hinckley. The following is a copy of the deed as preserved in the State House of Massachusetts.

"Know all Men by these Presents:

"That we, whose names are undersigned, and such officers appointed agents by the General Court of the Commonwealth of Massachusetts to make and to execute conveyances agreeably to a resolve as passed the fifteenth day of March 1805, and by virtue of other powers vested in us by the same resolve: For and in consideration of $9019.80 paid into the treasury of the Commonwealth have given, granted, sold and conveyed, by these same presents in behalf of the Commonwealth do give, grant, sell and convey unto Samuel Hinckley esquire of Northampton, in the County of Hampshire and Commonwealth aforesaid, assignee of Titus Goodman and Seth Wright, a township of land lying in the county of Washington and Commonwealth aforesaid containing thirty thousand, seven hundred and seventy acres to the same, more or less, the said township being numbered three in the first range of Townships lying west of the Passamaquoddy river as the same was surveyed by Samuel Titcomb in the year 1794—said township was originally contracted for by said Goodman on the second day of March 1795, bounded as follows., viz: northerly by number three in second range, easterly by number two in same range, southerly by township owned by William Bingham and westerly by the line run by Maynard and Holland, excepting and reserving, however, about three thousand acres in the easterly corner of the township first mentioned, and in the southerly corner thereof, bounded as follows, viz: Beginning on the southerly side of the township first mentioned and on the westerly side of the lake therein, thence running northeasterly to the northwesternmost part of Pine Island (so called) then southeasterly including said island to the northwesterly corner, of the one hundred acres of land conveyed to the Indians, then northeasterly by the land last mentioned to the east line of the township first mentioned then south to the southeast corner thereof, then west to the westerly side of said lake the place of beginning, and also reserving in said township four lots of three hundred and twenty acres each for public uses viz., one lot for the first settled minister his heirs and assigns, one lot for the use of the ministry, one lot for the use of schools, and one lot for the future appropriation of the General Court, the said lots to average in situation and quality with the other lands in said township. To have and to hold the aforesaid premises to him, the said Samuel Hinckley his heirs and assigns forever on condition that the said Samuel Hinckley his heirs and assigns shall grant and convey unto each settler in said township who settled therein before the first day of January 1784 or in case of assignment then to the assigns, One hundred acres of land to be laid out as will best include the improvements of the settler and be least injurious to the adjoining lands so that the set-

UNDER JURISDICTION OF MASS., LOGGING 11

tler, his heirs or assigns may hold the same in fee simple provided that the settler his heirs or assigns shall within one year after notice and request pay to the said Samuel Hinckley his heirs or assigns, five dollars and on this further condition that the conditions of settlement contained in said contract shall have been complied with which were as follows, viz., "that the said Titus Goodman shall settle in said township number three twenty families within four years, and twenty families more within eight years from the date hereof," and the said agents covenant with the said Samuel Hinckley that the said Commonwealth shall warrant and defend the aforementioned premises on the conditions and saving the reservations aforementioned to him, his heirs and assigns forever.

In witness thereof we have hereunto set our hands and seals this seventh day of February, 1811.
Signed, sealed and delivered in presence of:
George W. Coffin   John Reed
Charles Davis   William Smith
Suffolk, Boston, February 7th, 1811
Acknowledged before Charles Davis
Justice of the Peace."

It is not known what efforts the first proprietor of Hinckley made to induce forty families to settle in the Township, but there is no doubt about the failure of such an accomplishment. Massachusetts made a similar provision for the settlement of the new townships in many of the deeds which she gave of them. *Very generally in eastern Maine these contracts were not fulfilled—partly because a sufficient number of emigrants could not be found, and partly because in some casses the land was inaccessable. Hinckley, or at least the southeastern corner of it, was very accessable by way of the lakes, or west branch of the St. Croix river. In 1820, or thereabout, David Cass brought his family and settled in this corner, and possibly at about the same time

*"A Statistical View of the District of Maine", by Moses Greenleaf, Esq. 1816.

Baxter Smith and his family made a stay of a very few years. Both of these settlements were upon the three thousand acres reserved by Massachusetts.

This reservation was sold to William Vance of Baring in 1827. On November 1st, 1832, Mr. Vance sold it to Charles Peavy, and it has since been called Peavy Gore. In 1827 Massachusetts sold the lot of three hundred and twenty acres, reserved for the use of the General Court, to Judge Hinckley. In 1835 Mr. Hinckley sold the Township to Colonel Nehemiah Marks of St. Stephen. Marks was the son of a loyalist of Revolutionary days. Prior to that war the family lived in Darby, Connecticut, but it went to New Brunswick in the general exodus of loyalists. Neither Colonel Marks nor Judge Hinckley actively engaged in lumbering in this Township. It is doubtful if the latter ever even visited it.

The Township eventually passed to Colonel Marks' heirs and from them to the following gentlemen: Thomas J. Copeland, William Duren, Henry C. Copeland, Enos D. Sawyer, John G. Murchie, James Murchie, George A. Boardman and Charles F. Todd. These in turn became granters of it to F. Shaw and Brothers on August 4th, 1870.

Pioneering languished, but the business of log cutting prospered. In 1810 a dam was built across the stream by Alden Trott of Baring. It was placed about ten rods below the present dam. Since that time great quantities of logs have been driven through it each spring. Many of them have been cut from the forests about Hinckley, but the trees here have not been spared. On Bonney brook many logs were floated. Ninety years ago, says a tradition, "Natty" Lamb, lumber contractor engaged by the Todd Lumber Company of Calais, drove thousands of feet of lumber through it. The Musquash river and its branches, East Branch, West Branch and Amazon, were also used although they have little current. Thus there were comparatively few places in the Township from which logs, with reasonable convenience, could not be removed. They passed down through the lakes, or west branch of the St. Croix river, to Milltown, and thence, as lumber, to many markets both in America and Europe.

These early lumber camps were built of logs. The roof was of cedar splits and slanted somewhat, usually toward the south, to shed the rain and snow. In the middle of it was a hole about four feet square which was funnelled up for four or five feet with small logs or branch wood, and covered on the inside with clay. Under it, on the ground, the fire was built. In the evenings after supper the crew sat or sprawled around the fire to enjoy its leisure. Somebody was always the butt of a joke that was not allowed to languish until a new one arose. Nearly every happening in the few pioneer families within a dozen miles was of interest and in some magic way known. Many strange things occurred in the woods. Despite a robust common sense pulses were quickened, eyes distended by a recital of them. There were accounts of experiences with bears, wolves, moose, bobcats, muskrats, beavers, skunks and many other animals for unfailing interest. There was also, unfortunately, plenty of whiskey. Dominos was a favorite game; cards was a prime favorite but little indulged in because it too often led to quarrelling. Each camp was in charge of a cook who endeavored to maintain order. If he did not succeed he quickly gave way to a successor. The crews were for the most part composed of men from families of early settlers in eastern Maine. Sometimes there were a few Indians among them, and white strangers sometimes joined them for longer or shorter periods whose antecedents were only surmised. A Frenchman with a violin was often one of the camp inmates. Jigs and reels then sent their cheerful strains out through chinks and broad funnel to the somber lonesomeness of the frozen forests while inside the camp the music spirited away the fatigue of the day so that men rose on nimble feet and in the narrow spaces around the fire danced clogs and jigs and double shuffles and every sort of clever step that native genius could devise. Against the bunks and log walls distorted shadows kept pace with the revel.

When the early bed time came the men lay with their feet to the blaze. Those who were wakeful could look up through the log funnel to the stars. In bad weather the fire sputtered with rain or snow that fell into it.

Sometimes there were no clocks in the camps. The men arose when the cook called them. The usual rising time was four o'clock, but it occasionally happened that a mistake was made and the men were aroused an hour or two earlier. Such an incident was too unpopular to happen often. Breakfast consisted of pork, fish and hot bread. The latter was made of wheat flour, sour yeast and warm water, and was a delicacy that old wood choppers still speak of with deep appreciation. Dunderfunk was a favorite dinner dish. It was made of bread and pork cut in small pieces, mixed with molasses and baked in a bake kettle in the ground. Studjo was also liked. That was made of rabbit, venison or any fresh meat procurable and potatoes, and cooked like a stew. The early camps had no onions to flavor such dishes. The camps were hospitable places. Any man traveling about the woods on any business whatsoever—lumber prospector, wood chopper looking for work, a chance fugitive from justice, a mere restless ne'erdowell—always expected to be entertained and was almost never disapointed. No matter at what time a traveler appeared he was invited by the cook to at least share the next meal. It was not good manners to decline. If by any chance the invitation was not given the traveler hastened to the next camp and there related of the inhospitable cook:
"He never saw I had a mouth!"

The camps were often poorly supplied with dishes. Sometimes several men would eat from one frying pan; sometimes wooden dishes were fashioned and used.

*Hazing was practiced upon new members of the crew. One of the favorite frolics was to prepare a bucket of soap

---

*Joel Thornton, a driver of an ox team in the earliest days of lumbering on the stream told his grandson, Stephen Sprague, then a small boy, of the hazing practices and also of the splendid pine trees at Little falls.

suds and lather the face of the victim with it, using a camp broom, a crude affair of small branches tied together, as the brush. The unfortunate man was then shaved with a huge, wooden razor.

The Rev. Charles Whittier, a relative of the poet, was a missionary visitor to early camps. He began to make his rounds of this section of the Maine woods about sixty years ago. Almost yearly since then he has visited Hinckley, and has witnessed the coming of many changes in the wood cutters' camps.

The first lumbering on Grand lake stream was done near Little falls. Here was a fine, first growth of pine trees, giants in size and unintermingled with other trees.

Lumbering firms operating here were; J. B. Hall and Company, John and George Porter, Peter Avery, Peasely and Whitney, Burnham and Heustis, Stephen and David Prince, Gates and Wentworth, James Murchie ,Daniel Morrison, Claudis M. Huff, Daniel Tyler. Some of the contractors were Nathaniel Lamb, Stinchfield and Waldron, Silby and Stinchfield, Samuel Yates, Asa Crockett, Moses Brown, James Coffin, Edward Cass, William Cass, David Cass, Mathew Sprague, Joe. Sprague, Ezra Sprague, Eli Thornton and Joe. Pollis.

For shelter for the men who in the spring drove the logs through Grand lake stream there were three camps. One was placed near the dam, another at Big falls and the third near the mouth of the stream in Township 27. The dam was rebuilt from time to time. About fifty five years ago it was placed in its present position. In 1873 it was almost swept away by a spring freshet.

In 1863 a dispute arose regarding the boundary between Hinckley and Indian Township. The line between the two was resurveyed for the state of Maine by W. D. Danna. He established the line as it now is. All of the boundary lines have been remarked from time to time, but with this exception none have been altered from the lines established by Samuel Titcomb in 1794.

CHAPTER III

Squatters, Sportsmen and First Road

It was about the year 1820 that David Cass came to Hinckley. He was born in 1774 in Exeter, New Hampshire, and said he was a son of Jonathan Cass and a half brother of the famous Lewis Cass. *It seems to be impossible now to prove this claim, and equally impossible to disprove it. The Exeter records of those early days do not mention the birth of David, but they are not complete. There is no reason to doubt his word, since with all his faults he was not untruthful. Jonathan Cass, his father, was a blacksmith strong, restless, energetic. He won distinction in the Revolutionary war, entering it as a private and retiring a Major. **"He was of coal black eye and very commanding presence." He was sent to Ohio to take command of Fort Hamilton in defence of the western frontier from the attacks of Indians. It is probable that the young David went there with him, and there acquired at least a part of the distaste for Indians which he displayed here. A story survives that he had been guilty of some lawless act in the west and had fled from that wilderness to the more forbidding one of the extreme east to escape punishment. However that may have been, he had much courage, some consequence of manner and he knew how to pioneer.

It is believed that he first landed in Maine at Oak Bay where he stayed for a year or more making bricks. It is said too that for a time he was in the Miramichi country of New Brunswick. In St. Stephen he met and married Ellen Marsh, then a sixteen years old school girl living in the family of Colonel Nehemiah Marks. At that time he must have been forty three or forty four years old.

*McLaughlin, in his "Life of Lewis Cass", says that Jonathan Cass was in his twentythird year at the outbreak of the Revolution. In that age of early marriages it is not at all unlikely that he had already contracted a marriage, and was, perhaps, a widower when the war broke out, or soon became one. His marriage to Mary Gilman, mother of Lewis Cass, took place in 1778.

**"New England Historical and Genealogical Register."

SQUATTERS, SPORTSMEN AND FIRST ROAD

When these two paddled up through the river and lakes to Hinckley they had an infant son, Edward, and a daughter, Mary Ann, one and a half years old. They reached the northern side of Big lake and settled upon a bluff overlooking the water. Their first home was a log cabin. Land was cleared and produce and domestic animals raised.

The cabin in time became overfull of children. William, David, Jane, Stephen, Lewis and Sarah were born here, and were the first white natives of Hinckley. A frame house was eventually built near the cabin. It was a small shingled structure, and two or three small rooms were added to it at later times. There was a big stone fireplace in the main room where the cooking was done. This also furnished the only warmth in winter. After the family moved into this new house the old cabin was used for a pig pen. If stray travelers happened into the vicinity they stopped with the Casses. These would almost without exception be lumbermen. The situation of the family was lonely in the extreme. Mrs Cass seems to have had little save work, brawls and children to relieve the solitude. Their near neighbors were a few Indians on Governor's point and wild animals. At one time, probably early in the pioneering days, Baxter Smith, his former place of residence now unknown, had a barn near them where he stored hay cut from the natural meadows around the Musquash river, and he may also have had a house where he and his family lived for a year or so. Traditions are vague about him. Despite this interval when they may have had white neighbors Mrs. Cass said in her later days that there were many years when she did not see the face of a white woman. After coming to Hinckley she never left the wilderness even for a day.

It is said that David Cass had some slight education as a doctor, and not only prescribed for the ailments of his own large family, but was in demand when sickness assailed any of the settlers who at length began to grapple with the untamed lands of nearby Townships. It is probable that whatever skill he possessed was acquired in the rough and by places in which most of his life was spent.

In 1817 the first white settler, Moses Bonney, came to Princeton. He therefore became a neighbor only about eight miles from the Casses, but not very accessable to them. Samuel Yates came to the south side of Big lake in Township 21 in 1833. Two or three other families soon followed him to the vicinity and became neighbors, the nearest not more than a mile distance and all of them easily reached by a paddle across the lake. It must have been at about this time that Cass became known as "the General" and his wife as "Aunt Nellie." The latter was well liked by the neighbors, woodsmen and Indians, but the former was often cross grained and everybody in the region, save Samuel Yates, was afraid of him. Strangely enough "the General" stood in awe of Samuel Yates.*

David Cass weighed, say those who remember him, over three hundred and eighty pounds. He was very tall and of a large, powerful frame. Mrs. Cass was very small. She never weighed more than one hundred and five pounds.

Calais was thirty miles from Hinckley. It had in 1810 two hundred and fifty inhabitants. Across the river St. Stephen was a little larger and a little older. Milltown was close by. These places made a sort of metropolis, bustling and growing, which was a constant lure to the backwoods pioneer. Cass made many trips there, leaving his wife alone with her children and unprotected from any dangers that might arise. Lumbermen often stored camp supplies upon the Cass premises. The smell of them attracted bears. Upon one occasion when he was enjoying metropolitan allurements little "Aunt Nellie" walked the floor all night brandishing an ax to frighten off an enraged bear that was

---

*According to the "Yates Book" Samuel Yates was "a robust man, of powerful physique." He was a son of William Yates, an English pioneer who settled in Oxford county, Maine, and who was a hard working farmer on six long days of every week, and an equally hard working and vigorous preacher of the Methodist faith on Sundays. Moses Smith, Asa Crockett and Moses Brown, who followed Samuel Yates to the western side of Sand cove, Big lake, were related by marriage to him. The first was from England, the second from Deer Isle while the former place of residence of the latter is now unknown.

SQUATTERS, SPORTSMEN AND FIRST ROAD 19

trying to break through the frail barriers of the cabin.

Many stories are told of "the General. He was so strong that he could lift a heavy bateau to his shoulders as easily as an Indian could lift a canoe. He had a special enmity for Indians, and successfully terriorized them. On White's island in Big lake cranberries used to grow abundantly. One day, says the story, the Indians had gathered a lot of them when he happened to visit the place. He at once demanded the berries. Upon the Indians' refusal to give them up he set fire to the island, and burned the berries and much other property belonging to them.

Indians used to come to his cabin when he was away and freighten Mrs. Cass. They would steal provisions and whiskey. One day when they thought he was not at home he lay hidden. When two Indians came to the cabin he suddenly appeared, seized them, one in each hand, and dragged them to the lake shore. He waded into the water to his waist and ducked them repeatedly until they begged for mercy and promised better behavior.

A yoke of oxen were unable to start a heavy log to which they were chained. He unyoked them and with his hands twisted and worked at the log until he moved it.

In a dead fall trap he once caught an ox that belonged to Mr. Lamb, the lumber contractor. He dressed it and cut it up for the domestic food supply. Mr. Lamb thought that at least a part of the animal should belong to him. So he went to see Cass about it. The giant looked him over and then drawled through his nose:

"When I hunts I always hunts fer fur," an answer that was taken to assert his claim to not only the fur, but to all that nature had put inside it. Mr. Lamb allowed his claim.

He was clever as well as strong. Once he was imprisoned at St. Stephen for debt.* The next morning he was found comfortably seated on a bench out side the jail. It could not be found out how he had liberated himself. He was again locked up, but the next morning he was again free.

*According to the story St. Stephen was the place of his arrest. It probably was Milltown, Maine, or Calais.

Since no locks could hold him he was allowed to go home. Once, says tradition, he indulged as usual in much strong drink when he was in St. Stephen, and a lawless celebration followed. A few days later the sheriff and his assistant came up into the woods after him. He submitted to arrest, and got into the canoe of his captors. When they had paddled a little way into the lake he said suddenly in his usual twang:

"Gentlemen, can you swim?"

One could swim a little; the other not at all.

"It's too bad," said he. "I has fits—I feels one coming on. I might upset the boat so you'd better paddle to shore"

They paddled to the shore as quickly as possible. After landing instead of falling in a fit Cass took his captors, one in each hand, by the coat collars and forced them to a fence. He thrust their heads through the top rail, and jammed it down hard enough upon their necks to hold them. He then walked to his house a free man. There is some doubt about the authenticity of this interesting incident, but it serves as an illustration of the reputation left behind him.

He would go off on hunting trips in the woods, and take nothing with him but his gun, powder and a bag of salt. He would live upon game and berries and sleep at night without other covering than leaves. Sometimes he would collect as many as three hundred dollars worth of furs, a fairly large amount at that time. *These would be taken down

---

*The sort of pleasures to be had down the river, and likely to attract David Cass are thus described by John S. Springer, in "Forest Life and Forest Trees—Winter Camp Life Among the Loggers, and Wild Wood Adventurers" Harper and Brothers, 1851. "It would be difficult to give an exaggerated sketch of the drunken practices among loggers twenty-five years ago. I recollect that matters were carried so far at Milltown that the loggers would arrest passersby, take them by force, bring them into the toll house grog shop, and baptise them by pouring a quart of rum over their heads. Distinctions of grade were lost sight of, and the office of deacon or priest constituted no exemption pass against the ordeal, rather the rite profaned. This process of ablution was practiced with such zeal upon their own craft, and transient passers-by, that a hogshead of rum was drawn in a short time, running in brooks over the floor. The affair was conducted amid the most boisterous and immoderate merriment—the more distinguished the candidate the more hearty the fun."

SQUATTERS, SPORTSMEN AND FIRST ROAD 21

the lakes and river to Calais or St. Stephen to market. He would take a list of the necessities for the family and house carefully written out by "Aunt Nellie." If, after he had disposed of the furs, he resisted the temptation to conviviality he would return with every article upon the list. If he did not resist temptation he would come home empty handed and the family would resign itself to the consequent distresses.

There was often riotous merriment around the Cass home. Gangs of lumbermen coming up into the woods were always well supplied with whiskey. This was a regular stopping place where they often consumed a fair portion of it. When drunk they would dance and sing and perform many clownish antics. A favorite one was to catch the dog and dip it into a barrel of tar that was kept standing in the yard for the smearing of seams of boats. After a good coating of tar the animal was rolled in the abundant chips that littered the yard. After this treatment it ran wildly around to the great amusement of the men.

It is only by means of such stories that glimpses are caught of those early days in the Township. A certain measure of prosperity came to David Cass. He cleared about one hundred acres of woodland, and collected stumpage upon three hundred acres more. He raised pigs and found it a profitable business although at that time they sold for seventy five cents each. He kept six or seven cows, and two or three yokes of oxen. When he was seventy three years old his pecularities, which had been increasing with the years, developed into actual insanity, and it was necessary to take him to the state hospital at Augusta. The journey was begun by a paddle down the well known way over the lakes to Princeton—by that time a settlement struggling into village size. He was fastened into a stall in a barn for safe keeping over night. The next morning he was outside the barn although it had been carefully and, it was thought, securely fastened. Fortunately he had lingered in the vicinity. It was August 14th, 1847, when he was admitted to the state asylum, and on January

6th, 1850, he died there suddenly of apoplexy at the age of seventy-six years.

The care of the Cass homestead fell to the eldest son, Edward. He was unmarried, and, say those who remember him, was a melancholy man, conscious of his lack of education and his uncouth environments. He more nearly resembled his father in size than any of the other sons. Stephen also never married. He spent his life upon this homestead. Mary Ann married Joseph Hold, whose name became corrupted to Holes, and who came from Amity. They chose a spot on the south side of Big lake, in Township 21, near the narrows that connects it with Long lake and there lived lives of pioneering hardship. Jane, early married Richard Brown and left this Township to live in southern New Brunswick where her husband owned a saw mill. Sarah, usually called Sally, died at about the age of forty unmarried. She was a large woman, although not tall. She was timid, and often hid during the visits of hilarious woodsmen. Every member of the family seems to have been carefully weighed and for many years a record of the respective avoirdupois was mentally kept. This record is partly forgotten now, but Sarah is said to have weighed three hundred and fifty pounds. Lewis died in infancy. That only one of these wilderness born and reared children did not live to reach maturity is a tribute to "Aunt Nellie's" care and skill. William married Mary Todd, a reputed school teacher of Milltown. He settled west of his father's home, taking one hundred acres of the wild land. He was thriftless and his wife not competent for the duties that confronted her. In later years the family were in want. The last of William's life was spent in the house his father built. His own place was sold for taxes. David married Mary Yates, a daughter of Samuel Yates. He settled about four miles west of the original home and took one hundred and fifty acres of the wild land. It was in this very comfortable home that "Aunt Nellie" spent her last years. Her mind, like her husband's, eventually lost its balance. The hardships, loneliness and deprivations of this rough life might

SQUATTERS, SPORTSMEN AND FIRST ROAD 23

well have been its ruin. It is said that during the last years of her life she would take an ax to bed. Probably perturbed ideas of dangers long passed still haunted her— the bear she had warded off through a whole lonely night, the constant menace of bears and wolves*, visits of drunken Indians when her husband was away, drunken woodcutters and river drivers and the ugly moods of David himself. Bits of the past must have constantly passed through her mind like a jumbled nightmare of horrors. One day at noon she disappeared. She was never seen again although four hundred men, hastily assembled from far and near, searched the woods for her This happened in 1870, and to this day not the least clue to her fate has been found. A rather strange incident happened about three years after her disappearance, however, which may possibly lay open a subsequent bit of her life.

At that time Mr. Jackson Brown, one of the early settlers of the village, then recently and suddenly sprung into existence, lived temporarily in an old log camp long used by lumbermen. It stood on a knoll on the west side of the stream just above the dam, and perhaps six hundred yards from the clustered buildings in the village center. One evening in the winter when it was cold and clear a light crust had formed over the new snow that covered the ground. Mrs. Brown and several of the children were in the camp. It was very quiet around it. The windows were uncurtained. The family suddenly saw an old woman standing outside a window and looking in upon them. She was very small, not larger than a ten years old girl, says Mrs. Brown in describing her, and her face was deeply furrowed. She was so outlandish looking that a panic seized most of the family. They retreated to the further side of the room. She said nothing, but held up her hand upon which a white rag was tied. She stood for some time looking into the room,

---

*Once when William Cass, then a young man, was driving an ox team across the ice of Big lake with a sledge of supplies he was set upon by wolves. They jumped upon the load, and to save himself from their attack he rode crouched down on the pole between the oxen. This story is told by Mrs. Ellen Hawkins.

an unknown, disheveled woman. At length she went away.

When Mr. Brown came home the ground under the window was looked at carefully by the light of a lantern, but there were no tracks discovered upon it. That the thin crust over the snow was not broken seemed to confirm the family's belief that their visitor was supernatural. It certainly proved that she was very small and slight. To suggest that this woman was Mrs. Cass raises a multitude of obvious questions and doubts, and leaves the mystery of her disappearance still unsolved.

It is thought by some that after she left her son's house she wandered back toward her old home, fell into the intervening swamp and sank beneath its surface. She had often been known to attempt to wander back to the old place. It is more generally believed, however, that she was drowned in Big lake and so again found in the waters over which she traveled to come here the way to another unknown land, it must be it seems, of happier event. Many times she must have gazed at the sunlit, open lake for relief from the interminable shade of the forest; again and again in curiosity and longing her thoughts must have reached over this pathway to the wide world beyond her knowledge. Dimly her sick mind might perceive it to be the way of rest.

"She was very kind, a very dear woman," says one who remembers her.

Nathanial Scribner, his wife and three children of Jackson's Brook, now Brookton, made a settlement near the Casses in Hinckley. They remained there four or five years. This was probably shortly after settlers began to move into the Townships south and southeast of Hinckley—in the latter part of the third or the first part of the fourth decade of the nineteenth century. The traditions are too vague to accurately determine the time of the Scribner residence here. In about 1862-3, Edward Cass rented the homestead to John Robinson of Number 21, a pioneer near the Yates settlement. The Robinsons lived here five years, paying as rent part of the produce raised. In 1870 Edward sold to Delue Simpson of St. Stephen three hundred acres of his father's

SQUATTERS, SPORTSMEN AND FIRST ROAD

estate. Mr. Simpson raised here cattle, horses and sheep.

The last years of Edward Cass were passed in Township 21 at the home of Moses Brown.*

When the wild land of this neighboring Township began to show a few openings for the homes of settlers the sons and daughters of David Cass for the first time in their lives experienced a few social amenities. At the homes of Samuel Yates, of Moses Brown and others dances were occasionally held. All the settlers would attend and even the Indians would come. The hair of the squaws would shine with grease, and their best clothes, so far as they had any best would be worn. They often sat back against the wall, or stood in the background while the dancing was going on. Sometimes the music for these dances would be the singing of the company, and a clapping of hands to mark the time. Sometimes a fiddler and his fiddle would be in attendance. Sometimes the settlers would gather at one home to push through a special work too great, or too pressing for the usual family workers. These occasions had a spice of festivity about them. It was at a school held in a room of Samuel Yate's house that David and William Cass, both fully grown men, struggled to attain the art of reading and writing.

A few of the descendants of "the General" and "Aunt Nellie" still live in Hinckley, but none of them bear the name of Cass.

Ananijah Munson is another of the dim figures of the past. A few former river drivers, now old men, remember him first as the owner of a small farm near Princeton where

*Moses Brown and John Robinson were pioneers of Big lake who chose sites in the untouched forest a little to the south of the Yates, Smith and Crockett homes. The former probably came from Baileyville; the latter came from Portland, Maine. Wolves, which infested Big lake for several years prior to 1852, often prowled about these isolated cabins. To keep them out of the Robinson home a heavy timber was each night wedged between the chimney jamb and the front door. These two homes were abandoned after a few years. They were inaccessible by land on account of the surrounding woods and swamps, and the water approach was often impassable, especially for weeks in the spring and fall when the ice was breaking up or forming. The forest has now almost reclaimed the land that they cleared with great effort.

he used to drive a yoke of cows instead of oxen. For some reason he gave up this farm, and went to Stone's island on Big lake. Here he cut down every tree and bush. His plans for farming miscarried, however, for the Indians soon claimed the island and drove him off it. That he worked hard, although in ill health, is proved for afterward seven or eight tons of hay a year were cut from the island. One autumn he taught school, gathering his dozen or more pupils from the families of settlers around Big lake. One of his former pupils, now over eighty years of age, remembers being sent out to cut a withe for his own punishment. He got a good, capable one, but into the under side of it he cut deeply every few inches. By careful handling it was made to appear intact. The master took it, drew back his arm for an effective blow when the withe fell to pieces. The culprit was standing conveniently stooped before him. The latter was seen to conceal a smile. He threw the withe away, then sternly sent the boy to his seat. He apparently forgave him for the punishment was never received. All of this happened before Mr. Munson came to Hinckley. He seems then to have been an unfortunate old man. He had two young sons, George and David. Joseph Pollis, at that time a lumber contractor, encouraged him and probably helped him to establish himself near the dam on the west side of the stream. This was five or six miles from the Cass clearing. He was given the task of seeing that the dam was always in repair. This seems to have been a kind hearted effort to assist him for it is the only instance of the dam receiving such attention until recent years. River drivers made temporary repairs during the spring drives. There were even times when it disappeared altogether for Samuel Yates told his son that he used to drive logs through the stream when there was no dam. However in about 1845 Munson began to give it special attention, and probably continued the work for several years. His first home was a little dug out in the sand bank just above the dam, or below the present site of it. Later he built a shack on a spot between the present residence of Mr. Truman Brown and the summer

SQUATTERS, SPORTSMEN AND FIRST ROAD 27

camp of Mr. F. L. Atkinson. It is said that his two sons ran away from him while he was here. River drivers, it was suspected, inspired them. Taking a skiff or canoe they paddled down Big lake bound on far adventures. They are not to be greatly blamed for this. Attractive tales of the great outside world must have often reached their ears. Their travels were cut short for their father, greatly angered, went after them and brought them home.

Mr. Munson himself seems to have had some taint of the desire to rove for he eventually went to a small island on Grand lake. Just how long he stayed there is uncertain. It was not long, however. He was taken ill and a relative from Princeton took him back to that village where he died before 1853. The island received his name.

The next settler to come to Hinckley was James Dibble of Woodstock, New Brunswick. In 1870, just a few months before the Shaw brothers purchased the Township and began work for a tannery, he built a house, pyramid shaped, at Big falls, a pretty spot midway the stream. Here his son was born. He was the first white child to see the light within the limits of the Township's new village which was soon to come into existence and was to be called Grand Lake Stream. The child was named for two sportsmen, John Simpson and John Babcock, both of Portland, Maine, who used to camp near the spot. He was thus John Babcock Dibble.

Joseph Henry Hawkins, born in Lubec, Maine, and his wife, Ellen, (daughter of Mary Ann Cass Hold) made a small clearing on the north shore of Big lake just west of the William Cass place. They were married in June, 1871, and immediately began pioneering.

William Gould came to the northern edge of Township 27 where it borders on Hinckley in 1854 or 1855. Here, almost at the outlet of Grand lake stream, he built a landing which at once became the point of entry into the Township for sportsmen. For by that time the fame of the salmon in the stream was known to many zealous fishermen. Many distinguished men were among those who came here from all parts of New England, New Brunswick, New York and even from Pennsylvania and North Carolina. Sometimes as many as fifty tents would dot the woods along the sides of the stream during the spring season. A favorite site for them was on the east side of the stream. Beginning at the dam they would stretch a quarter of a mile or more along the bank. West of the stream the line was shorter, extending not more than a hundred yards, or from a spot near the present dam to another opposite the house built later by Thomas Calligan. Besides these clusters there would be tents scattered about in other places.

Two sportsmen from Massachusetts camped upon the stream at Little falls in September 1870 for about eight days. They were paddled up over Big lake to the spot by their Indian guides, Peter Sepris and his son Joe. It was a twelve miles trip. *One of them writes that they "took sixty-two of those beautiful fish averaging two pounds or better each." They made two or three visits to the dam where they found four gentlemen encamped—solitary inhabitants of the wilderness.

In those days tents and all camp outfits were brought in over the old Indian carry—at first on the shoulders of Indian guides. A sort of road was gradually worn over this route. Mr. Charles A. Rolfe of Princeton, who remembers those times well, says that it was the "worst old tote road" he ever traveled.

"Mr. Gould built a heavy truck wagon with long axles for the wheels to play back and forth on so that when one of them struck a big granite boulder it would slip in or out eight or ten inches and pass by the rock instead of over it," says Mr. Rolfe in a letter. "With that wagon he managed to tote baggage over the road to the dam, but no one ever dared to let him tote a canoe. **The Indians preferred to carry theirs on their shoulders. The guides were all Indians in those days—and were good guides too. Fishing was done on the stream only, and just above the dam. Lake

*Mr. J. Augustine Wade of Cambridge.
**Mr. Wade calls Mr. Gould's wagon a jumper wagon.

SQUATTERS, SPORTSMEN AND FIRST ROAD   29

trolling did not come into vogue until well into the seven'-
ties."

In all this time the "old tote road" of which Mr. Rolfe
writes had been the only one in the Township—unless there
were still rougher logging roads that led to forests fastnes-
ses. In 1867 a company was formed, the members of which
were Joseph Granger, William Duren, A. Halligan, L. L.
Wadsworth and others of Calais and Putnam Rolfe of Prince
ton whose object was to build a road which should begin
on the Houlton road, two miles north of Princeton, and
pass through a number of Townships, among them Hinckley,
to Milford on the Penobscot river, thence to Bangor.* According to a book written by Major Frederick Wood, "The
Turnpikes of New England," published in 1919, the charter
was given in 1863 and this "Granger Turnpike Company"
was the only one chartered by the Maine Legislature to
built turnpikes despite the fact that after the serration
from Massachusetts, Maine "adopted a comprehensive code
of general laws," to form road building corporations. In
his book Major Wood says that "the Legislature resolved
that thirty thousand dollars should be appropriated from
the sale of public lands and timber, and that as fast as the
corporations had expended thirteen thousand dollars of its
own money, the state should contribute ten thousand dollars
of the appropriation to continue the work."** The name
was afterward changed to "Princeton and Milford Turnpike
Company." The road was surveyed and work was begun
in 1869. It was in a very rough state from the Houlton
road to the stream when the Shaw Brothers began work on
a tannery close to the stream in Hinckley. Obstacles, both
financial and physical, had paralyzed the turnpike company's
efforts. Its difficulties were brought before the Legislature,
and in 1876 all public money set aside for its assistance was
turned back into the state treasury. West of the stream

---

*Information given by Mr. Rolfe.
**According to Mr. Rolfe $2,000 was to be spent by the state on
the road for every $2,000 which the turnpike company spent. This
seems to have been a later arrangement.

three or four miles of road had been "grubbed out" when the project was abandoned. If the road had been completed it would have opened a lot of new farming and timber land, and shortened the distance to Bangor, as it was and still is necessary to travel, by forty miles.

A few yards west of the border of Indian Township this road crosses the Musquash river, the waterway into the middle of the Hinckley Township. Swamps stretch on either side of it, and have been, and are, a trial to road makers. Many wagons have been mired here. The bridge over it is the subject of a poem by a local poet which will be found in the appendix.

The spot is wild, strange and gloomy. Early settlers of Big Lake came here when the land was frozen, and cut meadow hay, sometimes with the knowledge that wolves were lurking near. *Once two men who came over the ice o. Big Lake with an ox team to carry home a load of this hay were caught in a heavy snow storm and lost their way. They remained all night in a perilous, white, whirling wilderness, suffering with cold and hunger. In the morning, fortunately, they were able to find the way home.

*Jackson Brown and Milford Crosby of Township 21.

THE SAW MILL

Tannery shows vaguely to the right; the Company's office building is in rear of Saw Mill

THE DAM

THE "EASTERN," Prototype of the "FANNY BATES" and the "H. L. DRAKE," is above the dam

CHAPTER IV
The Tannery

The Messrs. William, Fayette and Thackster Shaw who put to rout about one half square mile of the Township's wilderness, were well known in the financial world when they undertook this new venture. They had already establish and successfully operated several tanneries which were scattered over eastern Maine, and New York state and there were even one or two in Canada. The tannery here became the largest and for a time the most prosperous of them all. "The Shaws learned tanning from their father who was a small tanner in Commington, Mass," says the "Boston Daily Advertiser" of July 1st, 1883. Their capital, when they first began business, was about $4,000, the same paper asserts. Business headquarters for all of the tanneries were in Boston. Mr. Charles Bates was a member of the local firm for about two years. It was then known as Shaw and Bates. Afterward it was the F. Shaw and Brothers.

Early in the summer of 1870 the Shaws came here to see if conditions favored the construction and operation of a tannery. The forests for miles around were thick with hemlock trees, the bark of which was then considered essential for the tanning of leather. The magnificent chain of lakes furnished good facilities for moving it to the foot of Grand lake while in the other direction Big, Long and Lewey lakes seemed to provide an easy and inexpensive course for carrying freight in and out of the place. The new road was another link with the world, and a preliminary survey for a railroad to pass through the Township near the spot chosen for the tannery had been made. Work upon this railroad, however, never advanced further than this survey, and the choosing of a name—the Magantig. Nevertheless conditions were such that a trade was concluded on August 4th, 1870, for the Township, saving only the reservations. The price paid was $35,000.

No time was lost in beginning work. Locations on the

eastern bank of the stream were selected for the tannery buildings. The course of the canal was marked, and other preliminary matters settled. That winter gangs of workers came hither with picks, shovels and axes. An epoch making upheaval began. In the zeal to do away with the forest not a single tree was left standing for shade or ornamentation in the new, small, ragged edged clearing.

The first workers to arrive found shelter in the old log camps of the river drivers. The first work undertaken was the digging of the canal. Twenty three Frenchmen from Montreal were the first to wield pick and shovel in the new ground. Three different contractors were in charge of this work. They were James Brown, John Love and David Johnson. The canal was about three hundred and fifty yards long, twenty feet wide at the top, fifteen at the bottom and four or five feet deep. It lay nearly parallel to the stream and provided a deep water passage from Grand lake to the tannery buildings. One of the first works was to build several camps, or log houses, until there were eleven in all. Each was soon overflowing with workers. A saw mill frame of hewn logs was quickly raised on the southern end of the bank thrown up by the canal diggers. This bank separated the canal from the stream. Machinery was placed in the saw mill, and the newly cut logs sawed into boards first for its own sides, and then for the other buildings that rapidly rose. Yet it was necessary to supplement its work by lumber brought up over the lower lakes on the "Captain Lewey," a small steamer.* A few feet north of the saw mill, where the Milford road crossed the canal and the stream, a long, high bridge of logs was built over both. The canal bank which passed under it was soon packed into a driveway by the loaded carts and drays that constantly passed along it from the dam to the mill. Many of the logs sawed were floated to the mill in the canal.

*The "Captain Lewey" is said to have been built in 1854. It retains its identity by grace of succession of parts, and is still used to tow tugs, and carry freight.

THE TANNERY 33

The mason work for the tannery was done by a French contractor from Montreal named Churchie. Two contractors, one named Walker and the other Peter St. Peter, framed the buildings and put in the machinery.

So eager was the firm to begin business that as soon as a building was ready the work for which it was designed was begun in it. Only about one fourth of the vats were at first put in the tan yard. They were increased one hundred at a time until in about six years, six hundred, the full capacity of the building, were placed and in use.

The completed buildings made a long array. A bark mill was placed across the canal nearly opposite the saw mill. Here it could conveniently receive the loaded barges of bark that were floated down the canal to it. Next to this was the leach house. Here the ground bark was made into tan liquor. Beyond this was the furnace house where the water was heated for leaching and other processes of the tanning. The bark pulp, after the tan had been extracted, was burned here and made a very hot fire. In the furnace house were eight boilers, and just outside it stood two iron smoke stacks. One of these was eighty feet high, the other sixty feet. A driveway led from the road, passed the smoke stacks and wound to the rear of these buildings. Loads of boards were constantly being hauled over it from the saw mill for the new buildings, small dwelling houses, barns and sheds, that now began to thickly dot the clearing.

This driveway divided the tannery buildings into two groups—the northern group, consisting of the buildings described, and a southern group. In this latter the tan yard came first. It stretched for six hundred feet by the side of the stream, and was eighty feet wide. When completed it had ten rows of sixty vats each. Two long passages ran down its length. Rails were laid in each for push cars in which the hides were moved up and down the building. The dry loft which came next was a huge tower one hundred feet square and ten stories high. At the top was a cupola in which a big bell hung. This bell called the men to work at six in the morning, rang for the noon recess at eleven-thirty, recalled the men at twelve-fifteen and dismissed them at six in the evening. The roll loft, or finishing room, stood at right angles to the dry loft. It extended toward the road two hundred feet. The beam room and soak vats were under the roll loft. The ample under ground sweat houses, eighty by one hundred feet, were joined to the beam room. Beyond the roll loft the hide shed extended another one hundred feet toward the road and nearly abutted it. An immense pen stock began where the canal ended and carried water the whole length of both groups of buildings.

These buildings did not complete the Company's plant. Simultaneously with their erection locks were built between two of the upper lakes, Sistadobsis (usually called Dobsis) and Pocumpass (usually called Compass). A lock was also constructed between Grand lake and the canal. A ship carpenter and his helpers were added to the working force. They built a freight steamer, called the "Fanny Bates," named for the wife of Mr. Bates. It was the first steamer ever on Grand lake. A number of scows, seventy to seventy-six feet long, and fourteen feet wide, to be loaded with bark and towed by the "Fanny Bates", were also constructed. There was a log store where a few staple groceries and other articles were kept; carpenter and blacksmith shops were established and other needs attended. Probably eighty or ninety men were employed in the tannery by the end of the first year, and as many more worked around the village on outside matters.

Thus quickly and thoroughly startling changes were inaugurated in the Township. The new village, although it was never named, was called Grand Lake Stream. From this time forward the history of the Township centered in it. The business grew until within its forest covered borders Hinckley had the largest tannery in the world, valued at $250,000.

*In 1872 a new boat landing was built on the north shore

---

*A small clearing at this point is called the "Greenlaw Chopping". It was made by Captain George Greenleaf of Calais in 1849 and 1850 because of the excellent hay that grew on the land.

THE TANNERY 35

of Big lake about a mile east of the Gould landing. A road was cut to this landing from a point on the "old tote road" about a mile and a half from the tannery where the latter road twisted westward with the stream. A large hide shed or freight house was erected at this landing. It became a very busy place.

Bark camps were established on the shores of the upper lakes, and in the deeper stretches of the forests. Two or three hundred men were employed at these camps in a summer season. Gathering the bark was an important part of the Company's business. In June, July and August when the sap was running and the bark was easily peeled, the black flies, mosquitoes and midges were a constant torment to the men in the woods, but nothing was allowed to interfere with their tasks. The bark would be stacked in cord and half cord piles and then yarded. If it happened to be on a convenient lake shore it was taken at once to the tannery. If it was inconveniently situated it and the logs from which it was peeled would, during the winter, be hauled to landings on Dobsis, Scraggley or Junior lakes. All summer the work of getting the bark to the village would continue. From lake landings it would be loaded onto barges and the "Fanny Bates" would tow four of them at once, two on each side, down to the foot of Grand lake. Sometimes it was a twenty-five miles journey. On Dobsis lake there was a boat called "Dobsis Loon" that helped in this work, particularly when the water was low. In times of special stress it made short trips back and forth on Dobsis lake taking the barges to the locks there where the "Fanny Bates" could more readily get them.

When the scows of bark reached the dam they would be taken through the lock. Some of them went directly to the tannery; others had their contents piled along the sides of the canal. As the business grew these bark piles were in every available place around the stream and tannery.

The work of bark collecting required many horses. In 1881, when the business was most prosperous, at City Camp, on Second Chain lake, fifty pairs of horses were needed to haul bark and logs to Dobsis lake. At the same time, eight miles away at another camp, eight pairs were used. Four miles further twenty four pairs were used. From around Scraggly lake at the same time, six hundred cords of bark were being taken which necessitated the use of many more horses. One hunrded pairs worked constantly in the village. Probably the Company owned and used four hundred pairs of horses for a season's bark hauling. Forty cords of bark were consumed in a single day in the tannery, but even this great amount did not furnish sufficient tan liquor. It was brought from outside tan extract works. Probably twenty-five barge loads of it a week were hauled over almost impassable roads to the vats of the village.

The hemlock logs from which the bark was stripped were floated down the lakes and streams in the spring. Those that were not needed in the village passed along to the lumber mills at Milltown. Log driving on Grand and the upper lakes was at that time still accomplished by the old fashioned method of a capstan on a raft. A great anchor attached to a long tow line would be carried ahead by men in a small boat, dropped into the water, and then the raft would be drawn up to it by winding the line upon the capstan. This work went on unceasingly day and night. On Big lake the "Captain Lewey" did this work.

After the tannery had been in operation about six years the drafts of the iron smoke stacks became so unsatisfactory that the stacks were taken down. Bricks for a chimney were burned at Big Falls where a brick yard was established. Three master masons came from Montreal to build the chimney. At that time eight more boilers were added to the furnace house equipment, and a whistle took the place of the bell. The latter still hung in the cupola, and was used on various occasions. One of these was tolling to the village the news of the death of General Grant.

At the time of its greatest prosperity the tannery gave employment to more than one hundred and fifty men at inside work, and as many more worked upon the bark in the village. Sometimes twelve hundred hides would be

THE TANNERY

finished in a day. All of these hides, coming in raw and going out finished, made a great freight business. Some of them were hauled over the road to Princeton; others were hauled to the landing on Big lake and taken down Big, Long and Lewey lakes by the much worked "Captain Lewey." From Princeton hides were shipped over the Princeton and Calais Railroad (then called Penobscot and St. Croix) to Calais. From Calais some were sent to Boston in steamers, but the greater part were carted across the New Brunswick border to St. Stephen. Thence they were shipped to Vanceboro by way of the New Brunswick railroad. From Vanceboro they went over the European and North American, the Maine Central and the Boston and Maine railroads to Boston. It was not only a roundabout but an expensive journey, and one of the contributing causes of the failure which eventually came.

The process of tanning at first took about six months. Afterward the process was completed in four months. The raw hides came doubled together. They were first put to soak in vats of water in the beam room. They stayed here ten days, were taken out, opened, split in two pieces, milled in the hide mill to soften them, and washed. After this process they hung in the sweat house for several days. This loosened the hair. They then went back to the hide mill to be remilled. By this time nearly all of the hair would have fallen off, but curriers took them and cleaned off any hair or flesh that might still cling to them. At this stage the hides were called green leather. They were then ready to soak in weak tan liquor. After ten days of this treatment they would be thickened and the pores opened. They were then ready for the real tanning. This consisted of soaking them in five solutions of tan liquor. Each solution was stronger than the preceding one. When the tanning was concluded they were called washed leather, and went to the scrub room to be cleaned of the tan liquor. From this room they went to the dry loft, and were hung there to dry for a week. Afterward they were oiled and rolled. They were allowed to dry for a few days, then reoiled, polished on a roll, weighed, marked and shipped.

The raw hides came from California, China, Brazil, Argentina, India, Zanzabar and other places. Occasionally, through accident or carelessness, horse, zebra and camel hides came in with the others and went into the indiscriminating jaws of the monster plant. Once, after soaking a hide, it was opened and a quantity of furs was discovered. Unfortunately they were then spoiled. Whether a lone smuggler had thus hidden them, hoping to sell them profitably, and his venture miscarried, or whether the hide had been lost from the goods of an established smuggling enterprise no one in the tannery ever knew—or at least it was not generally known.

The best sort of tanning was not done in Hinckley at first. The Company became dissatisfied with the work, and ambitious to do better. Mr. Edward Kennedy of Pennsylvania was sending superiorly tanned hides to the Boston market. The Company was able at length to secure his services as General foreman for all of its tanneries. He came to Grand Lake Stream village, bringing seventy-five experienced tanners with him. In a short time thereafter the hides sent from here were as well tanned as any in the market.

CHAPTER V

The Village

Nature lavished much beauty upon the spot where the village rose, but the builders of the tannery ruthlessly blemished it. After the trees were cut the land was burned over. It bristled with blackened stumps; it was full of holes where stones had been pried from ancient beds for foundation walls and other masonry; rotted tree trunks, long fallen, were ground and leveled beneath busy feet; homes of wild animals were exposed and ruined. There was litter and destruction everywhere. The first camps were clustered around the rudimentary tannery buildings—seven on the eastern and four on the western side of the stream. Near the place where the Company's little log store early rose a great outside oven was built. Great quantities of bread were baked here every 'day. The same cook presided over a kitchen nearby where men from two of the camps were fed. In some of the other camps hard working women did the cooking. These women were for a short time the only ones here. To provide sufficient food and shelter for the constantly increasing number of workmen was one of the early problems.

While the tannery buildings were rapidly taking shape the Company, with even greater haste, erected rough dwelling houses. These, like the tannery, were without paint inside or outside. Even after this urgent time the Company wasted no money upon paint. The interest of the Shaws in the village was financial. Whatever could promote the success of their business was provided. Consequently actual needs of residents were not overlooked, but it was not in their plan to cater to any esthetic tastes their tenants might possess. In 1871 they engaged Mr. John Gardner of Calais to survey the ground plot of the village. Land was set aside for a school house, a church and a cemetery, and the location of streets was indicated upon the plan.

The actual streets, however, were for a long time but rough tracts for the passage of teams. Most of the houses were set around helter skelter where it pleased the fancy of owner or builder.

By the summer of 1871 some of the men brought in their families. Among the first of these to reach the new village were Mr. and Mrs. Cushman Ripley, from Waite, Maine. Mrs. Ripley's first name was Lavonia. She was a small woman, but possessed much energy. Mr. Ripley is said to have been droll and interesting, but unambitious. They built a log house on the west side of the stream not far from the bridge, and Mrs. Ripley soon filled it to overflowing with boarders. Mr. and Mrs. Robert Grindle and their daughter and son-in-law, Mr and Mrs. Spencer, all of Brookton, came as early as March of that year. Mr. Grindle, who was a carpenter by trade, built a two story frame house (still standing) north of and very close to the store built at about the same time by John Fraser, a blind man, and his son, both of St. Stephen. Mr. Grindle's house was soon as well filled with boarders as Mrs. Ripley's. Asa Hitchings, of Moore's Mills N. B., became clerk for Mr. Fraser, and soon brought his family and lived over the store. In June Mr. and Mrs. Augustine McDonald came here from Waite. Mr. McDonald was originally from Prince Edward Island. They came up over Big lake in a sail boat, and reached the settlement at about eleven o'clock at night. They camped that night in a house but partially completed. The next morning a dismal scene of confusion and crude beginnings met their eyes. Yet they and others who early came hither seem to have had a remarkable willingness to bear inconveniences and disorder, and to keep in mind the bright prospects of the new enterprise. Excitement and hope came from the buzz of the saw mill, the blows of axes and hammers, the odors of freshly turned earth and of new lumber. Mr. and Mrs. McDonald's son, George, born the next year, was the second white child native in the village. The first neighbors of the McDonalds' lived diagonally across the rough roadway. They were two young men from New

THE VILLAGE

Brunswick whose family name was Linklighter, but whose first names are now forgotten. At that time they had a small house to themselves, but very soon they were crowded into its upper story under the roof, outside stairs were built for their convenience, while one of the many migratory families moved into the lower story. One of the Linklighters remained in the village nearly four years, and was the first blacksmith the Company employed. The blacksmith shop was a small, rough structure and stood between the tannery and the road not far from the Linklighters' house. The second brother, after a year or more, went away.

Benjamin Butler and two sons of New Brunswick were among the first workers here. Early in the summer of 1871 Mrs. Butler and a younger son, Martin, followed them hither. Mr. Butler cleared some land a half a mile or so west of the stream, and erected a house on the edge nearest the village. Somewhat later John Gower also attempted to tame the wilderness near him. Two brothers, Obed and Benjamin Fickett, and their families were among the early arrivals. The former became a lumberman and bark peeler, the latter a teamster. Both became permanent and esteemed residents. John Brown and his family of Red Beach moved here in July, 1871, and in August of the same year Mr. and Mrs. Thomas Calligan arrived and began the building of a home. Mr. Calligan became one of the first citizens of the place. Among others to reach the village in the first year or two of its existence and remain here were Mr. and Mrs. John Welch and family from New Brunswick, and Mr. and Mrs. Jackson Brown, with a large family of children, from a small settlement called Dixie in Township 21. Edward McCartney, a boarding house keeper of St. Stephen, came here with his wife and several well grown children and built and ran the first public house.

. . . .

After ten years Mrs. McCartney died. The care of the house fell to the daughters, but luck had deserted it. It soon caught fire and was burned to the ground. A new house was built upon the site. It is the large, weather beaten house just south of the Grand Lake Hotel. One of the McCartney girls married Henry Patterson, and they were the keepers of this new house. It remained a boarding house until the last days of the tannery.

. . . .

The Trask brothers of Springfield, Maine, were very early here. They built a log store and kept a rather large stock of general merchandise. A post office was established in this store with one of them, Lysander, as postmaster. A stage, driven by Mr. L. Lovering, a livery stable keeper of Princeton, daily took the mail to the latter place. It left Princeton early in the morning and made the thirteen-miles trip to the village and return to Princeton in a day if the traveling was fair and there were no accidents.

Traveling to and from the village was by way of the new road through the woods to Princeton in this stage or other conveyance, or by way of the lakes in a sail boat or canoe. Mr. Martin Butler never forgot the trip which he took over it with his mother when he was a liitle boy. Many years later he said of it in a letter to the "Calais Traveler:" "We ran the risk of breaking our own necks in driving over the new road to Grand Lake Stream, out of which the big granite boulders, some as large as a small cottage, had not all been removed." Mrs. Thomas Calligan remembers that in her first trip to the settlement she had to walk part of the way to avoid being upset by the rocks and rough ground. The "old tote road" and the recently made new part to the new landing abounded in stones, stumps and ruts. All of the roads were exceedingly muddy in wet weather, and loaded wagons often sank to their hubs. Bad as they were, however, a constant succession of carts and drays passed over or through them. Building material was coming in, and also furniture, machinery, groceries and everything the new community needed save fire wood and logs. Even then hides were being brought in raw, and carried out finished.

THE VILLAGE

A Mr. and Mrs. Dixon, who were for a short time residents of the village, lived in a camp on the western side of the stream. In the latter part of July of that eventful summer of 1871 the camp caught fire. So little could be done to stay the flames that not only that camp but another nearby, and piles of bark and cord wood, were burned, and a considerable portion of the village threatened. The fire swept down to the water's edge before it was extinguished.

French, Irish, Danes, Swedes—men from Nova Scotia, Cape Breton, stragglers from many parts of the world were drawn hither by the fast spreading fame of the tannery. The Company erected more and more houses, all cheap, small and flimsy. Sometimes two or three families of these foreign workers would crowd into a single small house, and perhaps find room for a boarder or two. Most of these persons lived on the west side of the stream south of the bridge. Here, in time, there came to be twenty-eight houses which belonged to the Shaws. There were also one or two owned by citizens. Mr. Trask's garden early gave way to them. The neighborhood became the scene of frequent quarrels and noisy festivities. It received the name of "Tough End" and has ever since retained it, although of late years without cause. A foot bridge crossed the stream near the southern end of the tannery for the convenience of these people. A great many of the first workers were unmarried men. Sometimes they were perplexed to find homes. There was scarcely a family in the village that did not take some of them to board. There were no unused rooms in the whole village.

The Company soon erected a large, although exceedingly plain, building on the corner of the Milford road and the "old tote road." This latter road was called Main Street, although according to Colby's Atlas its correct name was Water Street. In one end of the new building were the office rooms used by the Company. In the other end a large store was opened to succeed the log store. It soon drove the two pioneer stores out of business. The store of John Fraser became the Grand Lake Hotel.

As long as the tannery endured this hotel was used almost exclusively by tannery workers and lumber men. Asa Hitchings, the first landlord, sold it to William Elsmore of Westley probably in 1882. A year later it was sold to Joseph Jellison of Miramichi, New Brunswick, and in 1891 William Brown of Princeton bought it and ran it for sixteen years.

Mr. Robert Grindle sold his house in 1874. Several different owners each ran it for short periods. In 1886 it was sold to Israel Andrews of Machias. Mr. Andrews kept it twenty years and named it the Union House. It passed to his son-in-law, William Wilson, its last landlord. The house became a private residence a year and a half later when business in the tannery was suspended. It still stands but is in very bad repair.

. . . .

In the days of the village beginnings there were many minor insufficiencies. The advent of a barber, the opening of a school, even the opening of a small shop for the sale of soft drinks, confectionary and similiar commodities by the energetic Mrs. Lavonia Ripley were events of importance. The remoteness of this new settlement from any town of consequence made it necessary to meet here the needs of an independent if rather lean existence, and they were met with almost marvelous rapidity.

The first school was kept by a Miss Eveline Hill who came from Topsfield, Maine. It is said that the little boys were so anxious to begin school work that they helped to lathe the house. However that may be it is a fact that some of those boys grew up without knowing how to read or to write. After a year Miss Hill gave up the school, and Mrs. Stillman Sprague opened one in a log house built and used for a short time as a residence by Mr. Bates. She had here about thirty pupils. Two years later the school moved with Mrs. Sprague to a new house in the southern end of the village. In 1876 the Company built the frame school house still used. Mrs. Sprague taught here a year. A

THE VILLAGE 45

long succession of teachers have followed her. A notable one was Mr. James Spencer. In the days of David Cass and Ananijah Munson, Mr. Spencer was a young river driver and lumberman. He saved sufficient money to pay for a few terms at an advanced school, and afterward came to the new village to cast in his fortunes with it. He remained one of its citizens until his death in 1915.

The earliest church services were held in the log school house where Mrs. Sprague taught. Later the new school house was used for this purpose. Services were most irregular. Among those who flocked here for new fortunes was the Reverend Moses Gardener of Pembroke, Maine. He built a house in the village, but bought a little over forty acres of land on the north side of the Milford road at the extreme edge of the village. He cleared and farmed some of this land, but he also preached occasionally. Sometimes a young theological student would be installed in the village for a while, or visiting clergymen would occupy the school platform for a Sunday or two. Mr. Gardner or Mr. Gorham Gould (son of William Gould who built the first landing) read funeral services when there was no regularly installed minister. Though church services were more or less irregular a Sunday school was held each Sunday with Benjamin Fickett as its first superintendent.

Dances were an early and frequent amusement. A favorite dance hall was the second and unfinished story of a house situated on a knoll behind the present post office. This place was called Cross Hall, and was sometimes used for wakes.

Summer holidays were celebrated by various outdoor sports. A Fourth of July observance consisted of dancing, horse pulling, log rolling, walking a tight rope over water, wheelbarrow races, canoe races for white men and canoe races for Indians, swimming horses with men on their backs and many other performances of a like nature. At first "fiddlers" furnished the music for dances and other entertainments. At length, however, enough musicians were found to form a band. A band master was hired; one evening a week was devoted to practice and on every festive occasion thereafter for a period of two years the band was an indispensable adjunct. By the end of that time some of its members left the village, interest flagged and the band disbanded. Variety shows occasionally made their way in over the rough road. Whenever one did appear everybody, including the children, attended its performance. Sometimes on summer holidays or moonlight evenings the Company lent the "Fanny Bates" for excursions up the lake.

Drunkeness was common, although efforts were made to prevent it. In each deed given by the Shaw Brothers was the proviso that "no intoxicating liquor shall ever be sold, or a resort maintained for prostitution on the premises." Yet means of obtaining liquor were not lacking. On Saturday evenings a wagon, or sometimes two or three, came from St. Stephen loaded with intoxicants. These wagons would stop by the roadside in a secluded spot and do a thriving business. If, perchance, any of the stock was left it was placed in the care of a discreet person who usually managed to dispose of it during the week. If any employee of the Company was caught selling liquor he was discharged. Upon one occasion, at least, the St. Stephen traders were caught, and their liquor confiscated. On evenings when there was no special entertainment there was much loafing around the store. There was a large amount of business done in the evenings. Men who worked during the day did their trading at this time, and while the store was under the management of Henry Lester this part of the day was set aside for men, and no women were then waited upon.

A night watchman patrolled the grounds around the Company's buildings. These were, in later times, lighted by electric lights. The rest of the village has always depended upon candles or kerosene.

Houses now and then caught fire and usually burned to the ground. There was no fire department that operated on other than tannery buildings, but volunteers passed pails of water from the stream to burning houses. The tannery bell was rung for these fires, and the whole village turned

GRAND LAKE HOTEL

THE SCHOOL HOUSE AND MAIN STREET

This street has always been called "TAN BARK STREET" by village folk

out to watch them, or to fight them.

Occasionally somebody would be lost in the woods. The bell was then pealed that its sound might guide the wanderer back to the village. Searching parties were also sent out.

The cemetery was one of the earliest needs of the village. It was situated behind the eastern ridge that borders the stream. Here were buried many friendless, penniless strangers—human driftage that floated to this place. Their neglected graves are now sunken, unmarked spots.

There was no doctor, nor in the earlier years was there one nearer than Calais. There was no telephone, no telegraph. A doctor was summoned by the slow method of going for him. What with the bad condition of the roads, and the distance, much often vital time was consumed. Sometimes patients were taken to the doctor, but this was an especially harrowing journey. When a physician came to Princeton to reside conditions were a little, but not much, better. Most of the women were more or less expert in attending the sick, and prescribing remedies. At length it was discovered that one of the workers in the beam room showed especial skill in looking after the sick and wounded in the tannery. His help came to be asked in many cases of sickness. Suspicions were aroused by the expertness which he showed, and he finally admitted that he had been a surgeon in the English Navy and was a graduate of Glasgow University. Unable to endure the disgrace that had resulted from too frequent indulgence in intoxicants he had fled from England. He drifted to the village in the incoming tide of men. He was known here as Harry Spendlove. After his qualifications were discovered he had a great many patients, not only here, but in the nearby places of Waite, Topsfield and Princeton. He was provided with a horse and buggy for convenience in visiting these places. New clothes were given him, and he was otherwise helped and encouraged by the better people of the village. Nevertheless after two years of reformation he again fell into his unfortunate habits, and very soon left the village. Mrs. Robert Armstrong, sister of Mrs. Edward McCartney, living under the favorite dance hall, was said to be able to stop the flow of blood by the exercise of mystic charms. In 1882 the Company put a telephone into its office, and this shortened the time needed to procure a physician from Princeton or Calais, but there was still much suffering from lack of prompt medical attention.

Partly to amend the too prevalent drinking habits, and partly for social purposes a lodge of Good Templers was organized in 1872. The attempt to maintain such a lodge in the raw state of the village was unsuccessful. The lodge fell into desuetude, but was revived and reorganized ten years later. At that time George Sym was Worthy Chief, and Mrs. Augustine McDonald Vice Chief. There were about forty members, and the meetings were well attended. Permission was obtained from the Company to finish the second story of the school house for a Good Templers' hall. This lodge endured for twelve or thirteen years and met weekly in this hall. Debating was a favorite form of entertainment.

The wages paid tannery workers in the earliest days were about $1.50 a day. These declined after two or three years. Rollers then got ninety cents a day, beamsters seventy-five cents, yard men seventy-five cents, firemen, bark mill men and leachers each fifty cents. Bark peelers received eight or ten dollars a month and poor board. Later wages rose again. A dollar and a quarter to a dollar and a half a day was paid, and was considered excellent compensation. The rough, little houses rented at from two dollars to two dollars and a half a month.

The Township was without government. There were no officers of any sort save the night watchman. The Company kept what order it could, or when serious disturbances arose sent to Princeton for a sheriff. The village was singularly free from actual crime. Nothing is remembered more serious than squabbles, drunkenness and petty thieving. Improvident tannery workers used sometimes to steal bark for fire wood. They would cut trap doors in the floors of their houses and hide the bark under them. When the company,

THE VILLAGE 49

suspecting the thiefts, sent around inspectors no bark could be found.

It was the intention of the Shaw Brothers to set off one square mile of land for the village. Its southern and western boundaries were on the southern and western lines of the Township. The plan of the village made by Mr. John Gardner included a little more than a square mile. The settlement, however, never covered all of this land, although clearings did extend to the western boundary of the Township, and on the southern boundary was the brick yard at Big falls. The streets, according to Colby's Atlas, published in 1881, were, beginning in the west and running north and south; High, Shaw, Water and Main: beginning on the north and running east and west they were Lake, Bates, (on the east side of the stream only) Milford and an unnamed street south of and parallel to Milford. Only about one half of these streets have ever actually existed. Lake street was to cross the dam, but there has never been a public thoroughfare there. The plan of the village made by Gardner was the one referred to by the Shaws when conveying property. Nevertheless houses were built upon land marked in this plan for streets. William Shaw had a power of attorney to sign all conveyances. There were about thirty of these made during the days of the Shaws.

Despite the fact that so many persons owned their homes there was no residence of size or distinction in the village. The house built by Mr. Bates on the Milford road nearly opposite the Company's offices, the one built by the Rev. Moses Gardner on Water Street just below the tannery and the one built by Mr. Calligan on the west side of the stream near the dam were among the best, but these were all small. The roads remained bad. On the west side of the stream north of the bridge Shaw street was not laid out. People picked their way along through bark piles and rubbish. Tan bark was everywhere that a place could be found for it. The stream was covered with sawdust from the saw mill, and polluted by some of the filthy scrapings from the beam room. Some of this refuse, hair and rotted flesh, was used for fertilizer. Carts loaded with it dripped their contents on the roads, and an indescribable stench arose from it. The village was at all times saturated with this stench. The bare gravel bank thrown up by the canal diggers remained for some years an ugly scar. The rocks, pried up and rolled out of the way and the bark piles were its only decorations. In the zest to do away with the forest not a tree had been left standing for the distance from the dam to the furthest house. Yet gradually a few beauties crept into the place. Trees and bushes sprang up in places along the banks of the stream. In some of the dooryards fruit trees, cinnamon rose bushes, lilacs and flower beds began to show bits of color against the back ground of forest green, of gravel and of unpainted, darkening houses.

In spring, summer and autumn the constant arrival of bark from up the lakes, and its unloading, added to an activity which from the beginning of the village never ceased to be great. Loaded drays of hides were always passing over the roads, merchandise for the store was coming in, teams were busy with lumber or refuse, or in hauling the bark from piles around the village to the bark mill. Work, smell and confusion were ever present realities.

Men came hither seeking work in the tannery for whom no work could be found. To give them temporary occupation and support the Company established a farm (misnamed poor farm) a short way out on the Milford road. These superfluous men were sent there to clear and work land. Sometimes they were soon called to the tannery; sometimes after a short stay they left the village. They were in no sense paupers for they received nothing that they did not earn.

A year or two after the beginning of business in the tannery it was discovered that there was not sufficient water for the saw mill. To make a mill pond the course of the stream was moved to the westward for a hundred yards or more just above the bridge. This left a space between the stream and the canal for the pond. Two bridges were now needed instead of the single arching one that had spanned both

THE VILLAGE

stream and canal for the road space between them had been lengthened by the width of the new mill pond. The new bridges which the Company erected were rather unsubstantial structures. The one over the stream was well worn by 1881. One day during that summer when a load of lumber and shingles, drawn by a pair of horses, was on it it gave way and precipitated cart, horses, driver and two boys who accompanied him into the stream. The driver and one of the boys were lame, but they reached the shore uninjured. The other boy, Eddie Calligan, son of Mr. and Mrs. Thomas Calligan, nine years old, agile and well, was drowned.

A temporary foot bridge was thrown across the stream below the saw mill. This, though shaky and frail, was in use some time before the Company replaced the broken bridge. In the meantime it was impossible to drive to the western side of the stream.

CHAPTER VI
Lakenwild

In the second decade of the tannery interest for a short time flowed back to the neighborhood of the Cass settlement. Here a wildcat enterprise twined itself into the old Township's history. Mr. N. S. Reed, the perpetrator, began his ventures for easy fortunes in this part of the world by a lottery at St. Stephen. The lottery was lucrative, but the police interfered with it and it had to be abandoned. Mr. Reed then turned his attention to Hinckley for the quick growth and spreading fame of its village, Grand Lake Stream, was in some degree an advertisment for his own scheme.

He purchased about six hundred acres of land on Nemcass, or Governors' point for the site of his operations. Of this land one hundred acres were bought of Mr. Charles Rolfe of Princeton, and were the Indian reservation set aside by Massachusetts. Mr. Rolfe purchased them from Maine. and their improvements—a small clearing and house—of Peal Tomah, an Indian. Three hundred acres of the old Cass estate had been sold to Delue Simson by Edward Cass in about 1870, it will be remembered. Mr. Reed bought this land, and in addition two hundred acres of the F. Shaw and Brothers. With this estate, mostly marsh land or forests, and called Lakenwild, he was ready for the new venture. On the extreme tip of the point he built a handsome residence for himself. It was surrounded by a well kept lawn. He had a boat house and a substantial wharf. An elaborate prospectus, printed by a map publishing company of Philadelphia, his original home, showed this residence as the scene of a pleasant bustle. Around it spread Lakenwild carefully surveyed. There was a boulevard around the lake shore, and well arranged streets and parks. A splendid hotel was also pictured; steamers were shown on the lake; carriages with prancing horses helped to enhance the scene. It is probable that when Mr. Reed studied this engaging picture he sometimes forgot that much of this land, save where his own residence stood, was hopeless bog or forests and believed in his scheme. To accompany the prospectus, and equally attractive, were pamplets of descriptions and terms.

"Every lot faces upon a street and is so located as to take in the surrounding beauties of nature. Each lot has a street frontage measuring one and one half rods and extending back six rods.... Terms $2.00 down and balance in four monthly payments of $2.00 each.... If you wish we will build you a nice cottage from $200.00 to $2,000.00.. Send on your designs and we will carry them out..... Prospects of Lakenwild are brilliant in the extreme. Far seeing men of capital and shrewdness are investing in lots while many overworked, ill fed and plodding clerks, mechanics, mill operatives in town and city are taking advantage of the generous terms offered, and buying up lots."

In the prospectus lots were marked as reserved for schools, churches, lodges and other beneficent and social purposes.. Only five hundred lots were to be sold at $10.00 each, the pamphlet warned. The rest of them would cost not less than $100.00 each.

These advertisments naturally appealed to the imaginations of many "over worked, ill fed and plodding clerks, mechanics, mill operatives" and other struggling persons. Thousands of lots were sold. Notary fees and other expensives of the transfer made them cost their new owners about $16.00 each. Some eager purchasers took several lots.

Mr. Reed's mail came to Princeton, and so increased the business of that office that it was raised from a commission to a third class, salaried post office. He probably made, said a man who had been an interested spectator of this little drama, one thousand per cent on his investment.

A road was cut from his residence to the Milford road joining the latter near the eastern end of the Township. This probably cost him five or six hundred dollars. He was hospitable, and genial and well liked by those who knew him. Sometimes Mrs. Reed came from Philadelphia to make short visits. She brought a maid and many pretty clothes. The place soon became most interesting to the village people, but they did not invest in it.

The hayday of Lakenwild passed when purchasers came to take possession of their land. Someone remembers meeting an old man on the wharf there one day. The stranger was trembling; his eyes were wet. He had sold his house, he said, to invest in Lakenwild. It had been all that he had in the world. He had bought land with two or three hundred dollars of the proceeds, and spent practically all of the rest for a grist mill. He had expected to put up some sort of temporary shelter for his family, set up his grist mill and grind corn for the new settlers who, said one pamphlet, needed just such work done. He dreamed of eventually building a fine house, and of spending his last days in peace and prosperity. He found his land useless swamp land and no new settlers, nor old either, in the region.

A woman no longer young, put her few savings into lots in the hope of increasing them to a sum substantial enough to support her old age. Years afterward she wrote to one of the assessors of the village to see if enough money could not be raised upon her land to buy for her an entrance into an old ladies' home. Unhappily the land was worthless, and nothing could be done for her. This assessor received many similar letters.

Practically all of Lakenwild was eventually sold for taxes. But one woman of all the investors still retains faith in her investment, and regularly pays taxes on her lots. She has never seen them.

Mr. Reed's residence, and about six acres of land passed to different owners who have used it for a summer home. It is now the property of Mr. Morrill Goddard of New York.

CHAPTER VII

The Tannery Concluded

The failure of the Shaw Brothers was announced in the papers of July 31st, 1883. It was a large type, front page news sensation. Upon the same day, but earlier, the failure of C. W. Copeland and Company, one of the largest boot and shoe firms of Boston was reported, and was said to be the immediate cause of the Shaws' failure. Says the "Boston Daily Advertiser": "The first news of the embarrassment of F. Shaw and Brothers came from the return of the firm's checks from the clearing house endorsed 'no funds'. An hour's time after the regular settlement hour (one o'clock) was asked and granted, but although the funds at hand almost sufficed to cancel immediate obligations it was thought best to make an assignment..... The property of the firm in Maine, New York, Massachusetts and New Brunswick was made over for the sum of $1.00 'and other considerations' to Mr. Ferdinand Wyman to be disposed of for ready money in the best possible way that the proceeds might be devoted to the payment of the creditors of the firm. The assignment is dated July 28th.

An editorial in the same paper says: "The failure of F. Shaw and Brothers is the largest on record in the recent annals of Boston, and is an event the effects of which are likely to be felt directly in Boston, throughout Massachusetts, in northern New England and New York and in Canada... The firm of F. Shaw and Brothers was known to do a very large business, to have tanneries by the half dozen, bark by the hundred thousand cords and bark lands by the million acres."

According to local accounts thirty-nine tanneries and extract works were involved in the failure, and the assets were $5,262,000 while the liabilities were $7,500,000.

The losses of the village creditors of the Shaws were severe in proportion to their means. Probably no creditors suffered more. For some months previous to the failure little or no money had been paid in wages. Fortunately work was continued in the tannery; the store was kept open and domestic supplies could be secured there so although the prosperity of the village diminished its life was not extinguished. Employees of the Company eventually received fifty dollars each, and one third of all remaining wages due.

Mr. Wyman, as assignee, took over the business, and managed it. This arrangement soon proved unsatisfactory to the creditors. After about a year he was superseded by Mr. W. C. Clement, also of Boston, who was appointed trustee for the creditors. Mr. Clement remained in control of the business until work in this tannery was suspended in 1898. During the intervening years the tannery experienced various but always dwindling fortunes.

At noon on the 11th, day of May, 1887, sparks from the furnace fell upon the dry roof of the tan yard. Fanned by a tremendous wind they quickly burned through to the under side where the thick festoons of cobwebs caught and spread the flames. The roll house and dry loft were saturated with oil from the leather. The ten stories of the latter building were a perfect flue. The flames leaped high in the air, circled and twisted about the cupola; suddenly the walls swayed; the bell clapped a last muffled sound; then walls and bell came crashing down together. In forty-five minutes from the time the fire was discovered the tan yard, roll house, dry loft and beam room were in smouldering, flat ruins. The wind was from the northwest, and blew the flames away from the northern group of buildings so that they were not destroyed. The tannery fire department consisted of pumps and hose and was inadequate to cope with such a conflagration. The wind was so strong that the ice in the lake, still a foot and a half thick, was broken and driven to the foot of the lake. It was sluiced through the opened gates of the dam all day. It was one of the worst gales that the village ever experienced.

Insurance amounted to $30,000. As soon as the fire was entirely out of the ruins the work of rebuilding began. The cost of the restored buildings was $27,000. The re-

THE TANNERY (concluded)

maining $3,000 was used to build a new boat, the "H. L. Drake". This boat was completed during the winter of 1887-8, and took the place of the "Fanny Bates" already so well worn as to be unsafe.

The momentum, still very great, of such a business carried it successfully past the misfortune of the fire. By September, four months after the disaster, finished hides were again being sent out to the world.

Accidents in the tannery were not uncommon. Edward White, employed in the furnace house, was burned to death in this fire. Others had narrow escapes from death or injury at the time. Somewhat later Herbert Hanscomb was so severely scalded in the leach house that he died in a few hours. Martin Butler caught his right arm in the machinery of the bark mill. It was so badly crushed that it had to be amputated. Both of these men suffered grievously from lack of prompt medical attendance. The latter lay in the Company's office a day and a half before a doctor could be procured. The former's sufferings were greatly aggravated by the improper remedies applied by well meaning relatives.

On Sunday, the first day of October, 1883, a most peculiar accident occurred. The main boiler in the furnace house burst. The explosion shook the village. The air seemed to be full of pieces of broken boiler, rocks, bricks and other debris. One huge piece of fire box, weighing from two to three tons, was thrown into the air. It struck obliquely against the top of the tall chimney, took off a corner of it, and landed on the road three hundred feet away. The fourteen inch timbers of a flume in the furnace house were cut off, and portions of a solid four feet thick stone wall demolished. There was a sort of wooden bench near the front of the furnace. Several men were sitting on it when the explosion came. They were shaken off, and every one of them fell into a sluice way, and crawled through it to the stream from which they emerged unhurt, save for their wetting.

Workers in the beam room were subject to many minor

misfortunes. Loose hair from the hides would become embedded under finger nails, sores would form and fester and nails would drop off. In scraping hides the skin of fore arms would be rubbed raw. Bits of rotting flesh from the hides, or hair, would get into these places and make bad sores. There were always bandaged hands or arms in the beam room.

On March 19th, 1898, the old tannery was sold to the International Leather Trust, and its worn doors forever closed to business. It was bankrupt. The village it had caused to spring up saw junk dealers come from Boston and buy its useless machinery—its boilers, engines, bark mills, hide mills and rollers, shafting, piping and all its hardware. It was a community bereavement. In all, this junk amounted to two hundred and twenty tons. As soon as the sledding was good the next winter it was hauled to Princeton, and shipped to Boston. Sometimes twenty or twenty-five teams were used in a single day for this work. Thus denuded most of the old buildings fell a prey to the needs of inhabitants. It was a last benefit. Little by little they were pulled down, and the lumber carried off to make sheds, barns, pig pens and other shacks. Some of the lumber was used for fire wood. The saw mill, the bark mill and the furnace house were not entirely demolished. After a few years what remained of them caught fire, probably maliciously started, and burned to the ground. Even then the foundation planking, the vats, and other heavy material were left. Mr. Emmons Crocker, treasurer of the Union Machinery Company of Fitchburg, Massachusetts, bought all that remained of the tannery, including its site, and took away about ten car loads of salvage.

The crumbling stone foundation walls are still left; there are remnants of the partly caved in sweat houses, a little rotting planking, partly destroyed vats and the brick chimney. Stagnant water often stands in the vats and in the hollow where the tan yard was. Grass and weeds and bushes struggle up everywhere between planks and stones, and partly hide the ruins from the sight of one passing along the road. Nearer to the road on the higher ground is the immense chimney . Cows and horses now graze near it, or stand at rest in its shade. It is a land mark for excursionists on Grand lake, a summer home for thousands of swallows and a dangerous temptation for small boys. Several of the latter have climbed to its top. The chimney serves best as a monument to the past activities and importance of the village. Probably it will be less enduring than the low, crumbling ruins lying close to the bank of the stream and in the heart of the little sequestered community.

Mr. Charles Bates was junior partner and superintendent of the business for about two years. He then retired from the firm and left the village. Mr. Albert Clampert succeeded him as superintendent, or agent. He and all subsequent agents for the Company were locally called "Outside Boss", which meant that they were out side of or over and above, all lesser bosses. While Mr. Clampert was agent Mr. Henry Lester was manager of the Company's store. The business of this store grew rapidly. Not only all tannery workers traded here, taking up a large part of their wages in groceries and clothing, but it drew custom from the Machias river lumbermen. From it were sold from seventy to eighty thousand dollars worth of general merchandise a year. Mr. Clampert retained the position of "Outside Boss", for about ten years. Mr. D. T. Belmore succeeded him, and at about the same time Mr. C. E. Tarbox took over the management of the store. Mr. Tarbox remained in this position until the tannery was closed when with Mr. George Elsmore as partner he bought the stock of goods and continued the business. Mr. Belmore's stay in the tannery was short. After about a year he was succeeded by Mr. B. C. Chadburn who was the last "Ontside Boss."

The four foremen, bosses of the work in the tannery buildings, were successively, George Sym, of Montreal, James Kennedy, Charles Crockett and Thomas Welch. When Mr. Bates was here he also had a general care of this work. Alvin Doten looked after the bark after it was landed in the village, and Mr. H. L. Drake (for whom the new boat was named) was for many years the "Head repairer", called upon in all cases of breaks. Thomas Calligan was the chief engineer of the Company's boats, and had general oversight of them. Many times he was captain, mate, engineer, pilot and crew at once and so acting took the heavy, slow moving, awkward crafts up or down the lakes—sometimes in fogs, gales or inky darkness. Thomas Corry, however, usually acted as pilot, and was their captain. In addition to the steamers and scows there was a boat called a shanty scow. A shanty containing a cook room, dining room and sleeping room for a crew of ten men was built upon a scow. This crew of men loaded the bark upon the scows that were towed down the lakes to the village. The shanty scow was usually towed from one bark landing to another by the "Dobsis Loon" a scow on which there was an engine and a boiler and which was propelled by side wheels.

The failure in 1883 marked the end of the Shaws connection with the business or the village. They had never lived here. Mr. William Shaw died a year or two before the failure. It is said that if he had lived such a reverse might not have occurred. While he lived he visited the tannery twice a month. He would go silently through its various departments, note everything and afterward make such changes as were needed. Mr. Thackster Shaw was in charge of other tanneries and visited the village only at rare intervals. Mr. Fayette Shaw was chiefly concerned with the Boston office. After the failure he went to Philips, Wisconsin, and began a new tannery business. Here he was again unfortunate for a fire destroyed his extensive buildings in 1906. The following extract from the "Milwaukee Sentinel" shows, in the words of an enthusiastic reporter, the caliber of one of the promoters of the tannery which was here:

".... In company with Mr. Shaw I surveyed the ruins of his large tannery, the morning after the fire. Mr. Shaw said 'I am seventy years old. I have actively engaged in tanning leather for more than fifty years. This is the sev-

THE TANNERY (concluded)

enth tannery I have had purified by fire.'
' "Will you attempt to have it rebuilt?" I asked.'
"The bright eyes flashed with a new fire; the erect form seemed to expand, and I was greeted with:
' "By the Eternal, I am too old a man to be beaten in this way! The tannery will be rebuilt!" '
The paper further says that not only was the tannery rebuilt, but also all of the accessory buildings. Some of these were a boarding house, forty dwelling houses, a barn, store, and offices. They were all electric lighted and much attention was paid to the comfort and convenience of the workers. This was a great change from the methods employed in Grand Lake Stream village. The Philips tannery was but one of four at that time owned and operated by Mr. Shaw. The yearly finished products from them all, said the "Sentinel" sold for $1,500,000.

CHAPTER VIII

Hinckley Township becomes Grand Lake Stream Plantation

The F. Shaw and Brothers maintained the schools and the roads rather than pay the increased taxes that a plantation organization would necessitate. After the failure of the tannery the creditors, actuated by the same motives, promised and probably endeavored to meet this expense. The business dwindled, however; profits grew smaller and finally vanished, then losses followed. The last teacher employed by the trustee received but fifty per cent. of the wages due him. The people in the village made an effort to bear a part of the burden of maintaining the schools, but during the last years of the tannery their own financial condition was precarious. When it was attempted to raise money for school purposes by a popular subscription about eighty dollars were promised and forty actually collected. It was suggested that the school become a private one. Parents were to pay twenty-five cents a week for each child they sent; some even promised to pay fifty cents. Only a few paid either amount, although all parents wished their children to attend the school. Owing to this reluctance or inability to support a school there came a time when there was none. The roads, never well cared for, became abominably bad. It was, however, chiefly to make sure of a school in the village that a plantation organization was suggested and earnestly discussed.

The plan met with much opposition at first. In the urgency of financial pressure the Company had been obliged to part with the immense stretch of wild lands of the Township. Mr. J. P. Webber of Bangor had become their possessor, and he was especially opposed to the proposed plan. It was understood in the village that he offered to pay toward school expenses three hundred and fifty dollars a year if the Township would continue in its unorganized state. In consequence of this offer, or supposed offer, at the first meeting of the voters to consider the matter, July 1896, nothing was done. Several months passed and the school question remained as before. Mr. Webber's large donation was not made. A new agitation for a plantation government arose. Expressing the wishes of a majority of the voters Arthur Fleming, C. C. Hoar and Willis B. Hoar petitioned the County Commissioners that action be taken for such a change in the Township's status. Their petition was granted, and the following notice sent to Mr. Fleming early the next year.

"State of Maine   Washington County (ss)

To Arthur J. Fleming

Greeting—In the name of the State of Maine you are hereby required to notify and warn the inhabitants of Township Three, Range One, North Division, qualified to vote for governor, to assemble at the School House in said Township on Monday the 25th day of January at ten o'clock in the forenoon to act upon the following articles;
To wit.—

1st. To choose a Moderator to preside at said meeting.
2nd. To choose a Clerk
3rd. To choose three Assessors
4th. To choose a Treasurer
5th. To choose a Collector of Taxes.
6th. To choose a Constable
7th. To choose a Superintending School Committee and any other officers.

Given under our hand at Machias this 15th day of January A. D. 1897.

S. G. Spooner ⎫
J. B. Nutt ⎬ County Commissioners"
Geo. H. Coffin ⎭

At this meeting the following officers were elected:

James Spencer ⎫
Arthur Fleming ⎬ Assessors
S. A. Doten ⎭

T. J. Calligan   Treasurer

Frank Bagley \
Geo. McDonald / Constables

James Spencer \
T. J. Calligan } Superintending School Committee
J. Merrill /

James Spencer \
A. J. Fleming } Overseers of the Poor
S. A. Doten /

George F. Elsmore, Sealer of Weights and Measures

Joseph Fleming   Field Driver

S. A. Doten, Surveyor of Wood and Bark

W. B. Hoar, Sealer of Leather

William H. Elsmore   Inspector of Shingles

    Mr. C. C. Hoar was choosen clerk, and the above officers were sworn in the usual way before him, says the record. The meeting was then adjourned.

    The name of Grand Lake Stream was tacitly accepted for the new Plantation. A partial inventory of Plantation property in the book of yearly reports gives these statistics:

Value resident real estate	$ 4,726
Value non-resident real estate	54,688
Value resident personal estate	2,179
Value non-resident personal estate	169
Total valuation	61,762

There were fifty-two poll taxes, eighty pupils in the school, two hundred and twenty inhabitants, three hundred and fifty-nine hens and six dogs.

    Thus the new Plantation began its career humbly and without great wealth, but with great courage on the part of its few inhabitants.

    At the second Plantation meeting it was voted to raise four hundred and fifty dollars for a school, and one hundred

GRAND LAKE STREAM PLANTATION 65

and fifty dollars were added to this amount for books. It was also voted to raise two hundred dollars for repairing the roads and bridges. "By a vote the school committee was empowered to make some arrangement for a place to have school by buying, renting or building, and report to the assessors who can call another meeting if necessary." This meeting was adjourned for two days. At its continuation it was voted to give the work of tax collecting to the lowest bidder, provided he could give "the required bond, otherwise to be given to the next lowest bidder." The list of bids is as follows;

George G. Elsmore	4 cents 4 mills
A. J. Fleming	4 cents
Charles Fleming	3 cents 6 mills
William Elsmore	3 cents 5 mills

William Elsmore and Charles Fleming failed to give the required bond, and A. J. Fleming became the first tax collector of the Plantation.

Pursuant the recommendation of the committee appointed at the first session of this meeting the Plantation purchased and repaired the old school house built by the Shaw Brothers. This building, with all tannery property, had passed into the possession of the Shaws' creditors. Its purchase overtaxed the slender financial resources of the impecunious community. There was too little money left in its treasury to fully pay for the necessary repairs, and the roof was reshingled by volunteer labor.

The first taxes raised amounted to seven hundred and forty dollars and ninety six cents. Mr. Webber refused to recognize the Plantation organization, and for a time withheld his taxes. In consequence the Plantation found the utmost difficulty in maintaining its schools and in meeting the running expenses of its government, and upkeep. Its credit was so poor that sometimes supplies for the school were charged to responsible citizens instead of to the Plantation.

On April 12th, 1897, a Board of Health was appointed

by the municipal officers. The members were:

Stephen Yates	3 years
Willis B. Hoar	2 years
George G. Elsmore	1 year

This and all subsequent boards of health have found little, to do.

On April 27th, of the same year the voters petitioned the Commissioners of Washington County to "take such measures as will be found necessary in the earliest possible time to lay out and build a road across the lands of John P. Webber as follows: Beginning at the eastern side of the Plantation near the residence of H. H. Miller, running a southwest course over the line of road traveled to the village, crossing Grand lake stream above the tannery, thence to the place known as the John Gower place—such road being a public necessity." This petition was signed by C. C. Hoar (the clerk) and eighteen others, and was granted.

The Milford and Princeton road will be recognized in this description, the only land exit or entrance of the village. Little or no money had been spent on it for several years, and its condition was exceedingly bad. The Miller residence was on the eastern edge of the Township, and the Grower place about a quarter of a mile west of the stream.

On July 6th, 1900, a Plantation meeting was called to "instruct the assessors of Grand Lake Stream as to what they should do in relation to the N. S. Read property, known as Lakenwild, and the timberlands of Hinckley Township, owned by John P. Webber and son, all of which property has been sold for taxes." The assessors were authorized to "sell or convey to any party or parties any right which the inhabitants of said Grand Lake Stream Plantation now possess in any property that has been forfeited to the inhabitants of said Grand Lake Stream Plantation by reason of non-payment of taxes."

In connection with this tax sale of the Webber lands there is a rather interesting incident. Mr. Alden D. Hall, a stranger in the village, paid the taxes (slightly over three thousand dollars) and secured a deed of the whole great property in the expectation of thus owning it. Later when the differences between Mr. Webber and the Plantation were explained and settled the former redeemed his land, and Mr. Hall's venture came to naught.

Since the organization, and particularly since the misunderstanding with Mr. Webber has been cleared, the Plantation has, with such help as the state gives, maintained good schools. The public lots set aside by Massachusetts in the deed of the Township given to Samuel Hinckley yielded in the first years after the organization $76.60 a year. According to a report of the state treasurer made in 1919 the amounts credited to the Plantation from the sales of wood from these public lots are as follows:

June 1, 1850	County Agent	$192.49
Dec. 25, 1850	County Agent	141.44
May 1, 1850	Land Agent	112.25
June 19, 1851	County Treasurer	160.64
Total		606.82
	Debited	
Dec. 1, 1849	Expense County Agent	$23.16
June 19, 1851	Expense County Tr.	236.58
Total		261.74
	Balance	345.08

A further credit of $5871.88 was given the Plantation on July 1st, 1915. The principal at the present time therefore is $6216.96.

Mistakes have been made in this account. Thus in 1897 interest on $345.08 at 6 per cent for forty-five years was illegally added to the principal, and interest paid the Plantation on a Land Reserve fund of $1276.80. Thus while the Plantation actually received $76.60 a year it was entitled to but $20.70. These large over payments of interest have now absorbed all of the $931.72 ((6 per cent.

interest on $345.08 for forty-five years) which had accumulater during the years the Township was unorganized.*

The right to cut grass and timber on these lots was first sold by the state to one Stephen Emerson in 1850. The lots set apart in the deed for the first settled minister and for uses of the ministry were in Hinckley, as in many other Townships, turned over to the uses of the schools. The Plantation now receives four per cent. yearly interest on this fund.

In 1912 a class C High school was established in the much used school hall. In 1911 four hundred and fifty dollars were appropriated for repairs on the school house, and this included the expense of preparing the building for the new school. A small school in the Cass district was established soon after the Plantation was organized, but this was discontinued in 1914 there being by that time no children in the district to attend it.

In 1910 it was necessary to buy a plot of ground for a new cemetery. A lot on the Milford road was chosen. It is nearly opposite the farm cleared by the Rev. Moses Gardner. It was cleared by Daniel Campbell of Prince Edward's Island in earlier days, later sold to Charles Tarbox and contains about three quarters of an acre of land. It cost the Plantation fifty dollars, fences and other improvements have brought the cost up to two hundred dollars.

The Plantation has kept and put in good repair its roads. At present about nine hundred dollars are usually spent each year for this purpose. The Plantation raises one third of this amount and the state contributes two thirds. In 1913 a machine for grading the roads was purchased for two hundred and thirty-five dollars. Since 1912

*For many years the Plantation was actually paid $67.97 annual interest, a wrong computation on a principal of $1,276.80. In November 1908 this mistake was rectified by a payment to the treasurer of the Plantation of $156.97—error of $8.93 for each year since 1899 and interest of $76.60 for the current year.

It is believed that there may have been cuttings from these lots between the years 1851 and 1915 not recorded.

GRAND LAKE STREAM PLANTATION 69

Charles P. W. Calligan has been in charge of road repairing and has done most excellent work.*

In 1913 the Plantation bought a chemical, fire fighting machine, for which it paid three hundred dollars.

The Plantation has never paid much for the support of its poor, and it has never been necessary to have a poor farm. In many years nothing has been raised nor spent for indigent persons. In one year the money thus used was but fifty cents; in another it was a dollar and a half. During the earlier and struggling years of the Plantation's existence the poor were a slight burden. In one of these years two hundred and fifty dollars were appropriated, but not quite all spent. In twenty years the whole amount used for needy residents has not been over a thousand dollars. This is partly due to the neighborly, even family feeling the people have for each other. By this time by much intermarriage they are nearly all related. Everybody helps whoever is in trouble, and such help is never considered a charity.

The bridge which eventually replaced the one broken in 1882 became unsafe. New stone piers were built in the fall of 1917, and it is hoped to have a steel floor laid over them in a few years. There is a temporary but substantial plank flooring there now.

The political bias of the Plantation is shown by this excerpt from the clerk's book.

"In September elections for Governor, Senator, Representative and other officers twenty-eight votes were polled as follows:

---

*It has already been told (Chapter V) how helter skelter was the selection of house lots in early days. Some houses stand where the street should be; others partly intrude upon public ways. The following extracts from the Town Records are interesting. "It was voted that the town exchange a strip of land 3 rods wide with J. D. Sprague to save putting a street through his house lot." March 1915.

In March 1909 Abraham McArthur and others petitioned that Shaw Street be opened south of Milford road. The road way was occupied by cottages owned by Mr. Rose. A private way was accepted in lieu of the public one desired upon Mr. Rose's promise to maintain it free of expense to the village.

Straight Republican	18
Split Republican	2
Straight Democratic	6
Straight Prohibition	1
Defective	1

In March, 1917, values in the Plantation were as follows

Resident real estate	$17,660
Resident personal estate	6,190
Non-resident real estate	87,170
Non-resident personal estate	2,970
Total	113, 990

Non residents have built five summer camps which have greatly increased the last two valuations. In 1917 there were sixty-seven poll taxes at two dollars each, thirty-eight dog licenses at one dollar each. The highest amount ever raised by the Plantation in taxes was $3,557 in 1913. The lowest amount reported on the records was $450. This was raised in 1906.

Many of the details here set down seem trivial and perhaps uninteresting—the small affairs of a small community. In them are seen, however, some of the deeper and more vital roots of American respect for education and law. The establishment of a town government, its many officials, its orderly process and its resources and expenditures are studies in American rural life and conditions. Despite improvements the Plantation's financial standing has not yet reached a point where the strictest economy can be disregarded, or even all needs supplied. The school house, for instance, is practically worn out, but there are no funds for a new one, or even enough to make all needful repairs.

BOYNTON'S CAMPS
(Property Grand Lake Stream Company)

TREADWELL'S CAMPS

CHAPTER IX
Later Days in the Village

During the declining years of the tannery the population of Grand Lake Stream slowly dwindled. After the tannery's final breakdown there was an exodus that left the village about one half its former size. The census of 1900 gives the population as two hundred and twenty-one while in more prosperous days there were nearly five hundred people here.

The village property of the erstwhile Company, with the exception of the tannery and its site, was bought at a sheriff's sale by F. A. Wyman who paid, according to rumor by law services. Mr. Wyman sold houses and house lots to those residents who cared to risk their future in the apparently ruined village. These houses, it will be remembered, were small and poorly made. They were without paint inside or outside, save in a few cases where tenants had painted a room or two. All were without any but the most primitive conveniences. They now sold with a small plot of land at from fifty to one hundred and fifty dollars each according to the location and the amount of land. The original plan of the village provided for lots five rods across the front and eight rods deep, or just one quarter acre of land, and nearly all of the lots sold by Mr. Wyman were of this size. A few of the earlier settlers had long owned their homes, and two or three had acquired sufficient land for farming. After this sale the shrunken village became one almost exclusively of home owners. The new proprietors improved their property according to their means and taste. Barns, ells, sheds, henhouses were made from the free lumber of the demolished tannery; new vegetable gardens were planted; a few fruit trees were set out; cows and hens were bought. A few of the necessities of life were thus secured, but money to procure others was difficult to obtain. The outlook was exceedingly dark. In this extremity the natural resources and advantages of the spot were given a new consideration. During the hurly-burly of the tannery years some sportsmen still came yearly, but the place was unattractive then. The salmon in the lake and stream were very plentiful, however. One of the older residents tells this story:

"An old fellow in the tannery—worked from six to six—used to go up above the dam after supper with a cedar pole. He had pork rind for bait. He'd catch more'n he could carry home in no time at all—it's God's truth."

In the canal boys would "gig" salmon all day long. Big fish were often crushed in the mill wheels.

"It was nothing for a sport to catch one hundred in a day," says an old lady who has been here since the summer of 1871.

Energetic minds began to devise ways to attract more sportsmen hither. From the earliest village days certain housekeepers had opened their homes for the accommodation of one or more of these periodical visitors. Mrs James Forbes,* who with Mr. Forbes came to the village from New Brunswick in 1874, Mrs. T. J. Calligan and Mrs Benjamin Fickett were some of these housekeepers. Mrs. Lavonia Ripley's boarding house was the first one to make special provision for sportsmen. Her first home of logs was burned. A frame house was erected on its site and was one of the largest in the village. Soon after Mr. Bates (for a short time partner of the Shaws) left the place Mrs. F. A. Sym (Mrs George Sym) took the house built for him and turned it into a boarding house. She called this place the "White House." Following Mrs. Ripley's successful venture she too made special provisions for sportsmen. Several of them annually visited her. As early as 1893 Mr. W. G. Rose opened a Sporting Camp. He called it "Ouananiche Lodge." The house formerly belonged to his father who had been an occasional and favorite host to sportsmen. It is well situated on a knoll on the west side

---

*In one of the earlier days of the village a bear came out of the woods from behind Mrs. Forbes' house, entered her kitchen, tipped over and broke her molasses jug and lapped up the contents.

LATER DAYS IN THE VILLAGE

of the stream, and is one of the few spots in the village from which the lake can be seen. After the collapse of the tantery Mr. Rose gave the business a new impetus. Many new visitors were attracted to his camp. A number of small houses, formerly tannery property, were bought of Mr. Wyman, moved near it and renovated for sleeping quarters. After Mrs. Ripley's death Mr. Rose bought her house— which is opposite "Ouananiche Lodge" but on lower ground —and used it as an annex to the camp. He called it "Pioneer Inn" in honor of Mrs. Ripley's pioneer efforts in providing for the comfort of sportsmen. Eventually Mr. Rose organized the "Grand Lake Stream Company" to take over the business. Ex-Comodore E. P. Boynton of the Boston Yacht Club was made president, and Mr. Rose became secretary and manager. In 1918 the "Pioneer Inn" was sold to Alonzo Woodward, and so is no longer a part of this camp property.

Mr. Stephen Yates was almost as early in the new business as Mr. Rose. Mr. Yates is a son of Samuel Yates, the first pioneer of Township 21. In 1895 he bought the "White House" of Mrs. Sym. The number of sportsmen yearly visiting it presently increased. After two years, however, Mr. Yates was obliged to give up business on account of the poor health of Mrs. Yates. Mr. and Mrs. Frank Ball took the house September 1st, 1901. Mr. Ball came from Andover, Massachusetts, although for five years prior to this time he had been at the Duck Lake Club on Grand lake. Mr. and Mrs, Ball have enlarged the "White House," and built a number of small, attractive cottages and a garage. The camp is one of the most popular in eastern Maine.

Urged by former guests Mr. Yates, after a few years, opened another camp. This is an adaptation and enlargement of one of the older of the village houses, and it is well located on the higher part of the easterly ridge that overlooks the stream. He also has been obliged to build supplementary, small cottages. On April 30th, 1920, Mr.

Benn Treadwell, of Tuckahoe, New York, bought this property and named it "Grand Lake Camps." New and attractive cottages are to be built.

In September, 1907, the Grand Lake Hotel became the property of Mr. Alonzo Woodward of Springfield, Maine. In 1912 it was sold to Mr. Charles Bradford of Endfield, Maine. Sportsmen often stop here.

Thus the village has turned from the humble task of providing sole leather for the world to the pleasanter task of catering to its pleasures and its health. The men are nearly all guides. They are experts in fish lore and woodcraft. In the winters they work in the lumber camps of the vicinity. Between seasons some of the more enterprising make canvas canoes, ax handles and paddles. Some of the men are employed each season in log driving. The logs, hauled upon the ice in the winter and left to float when the ice melts, or yarded upon lake shores and rolled into the water in the spring, are collected into booms at the head of Grand Lake and towed to its foot. They are then sluiced through the opened gates of the dam, and floated down the stream to Big lake where they are again collected into booms for the rest of their journey. Jams, which form in the stream, often test the muscles and nerves of the men who liberate them by the skillful use of pevies.

The women and girls of the village are industrious pickers of the wild berries in which the Plantation is rich. In the summer they often help in the public camps, or in the private camps of summer residents.

*Dr. Samuel Mixter of Boston built the first private summer cottage in the village in 1904. A year later Mr. Arthur Blake of Concord, Massachusetts, bought a small house of Frank Elsmore, then a resident here, and adapted it for summer use. Four years later it was burned to the ground. Mr. Blake then built a summer cottage, and acquired in addition to the Elsmore lot three lots adjacent to it. In 1910

---

*The visits of Dr. Mixter and his sons have brought blessings to many afflicted folk here. No charge is made or care spared those who are ill.

LATER DAYS IN THE VILLAGE 75

this land and cottage were sold to Mr. J. B. McCoy of East Orange, New York. Since 1916 Mr. McCoy has been a permanent resident of the village. Mr. James T. Maxwell of Saugaties, New York, built a summer home here in 1909, and two years later Prof. J. W. White of Harvard University and Mr. F. L. Atkinson of Newburyport, Massachusetts, each built cottages. Two sportsmen from Brockton, Massachusetts, L. C. Thomas and H. L. Allen, built a cottage on a small peninsula about two miles from the village on the east side of Grand lake. This cottage was built in 1907 and in 1914 sold to Mr. Henry Nickerson of Cohasset, Massachusetts. Mr. James Brite of New York now owns the old William Cass place. He built, in the summer of 1919, a summer camp on Munson's Island, Grand lake. This latter camp is in Township 6 where it borders on Hinckley.

The opening of the Washington County railroad in 1898 has proved to be a factor in the new fortunes of the village. Travel hither from points west was, in the past days, roundabout, tiresome and expensive. It is now comparatively easy. In the spring travelers may, if they desire, still come in from Princeton by the old route over the lakes. A small steamer makes the trip daily when the water in Big lake is sufficiently high. Princeton is still the nearest railroad station, but the horse stage has been replaced by a Ford car—save in the winter months, and the road is now kept in very good condition.

Mr. Emmons Crocker who bought the remnants of the tannery and its site sold the latter to the Grand Lake Stream Company, and this company sold it to the St. Croix Paper Company, its present owners. In the general shifting of village property ownership at about the beginning of this century the Grand Lake Stream Company became possessed of the office and store building of the former tannery Company and the land upon which it stood. The stock of goods of the store was bought by George Elsmore and Charles Tarbox. These two conducted the business of storekeeping for several years. Then the partnership was dissolved and Mr. Elsmore became sole proprietor. The building caught fire and burned to the ground on the night of November 2nd, 1913. The whole village was lighted by the flames.

Some years before this fire, however, Mr. Elsmore ceased to have a monopoly of business. In 1903 Mr. Willis B. Hoar opened a competing store for the sale of general merchandise. Mr. Hoar came to the village in 1881 and became an employe of the company, first in the tannery and then in its store. He began business for himself in a small building near the Grand Lake Hotel and presently was obliged to add to it a large, front shop.

The spring following the disastrous fire Mr. Elsmore erected a small building opposite the site of his former business and there for a short time resumed trade. In 1915 Mr. Robert Sutherland opened a store in this building. Groceries, dry goods, boots and shoes and hardware are all here as in the store of Mr. Hoar. Several other essays at store keeping have been of short duration and more or less successful.

The Grand Lake Stream Company erected a slightly smaller building than the old tannery office building upon the site of the latter. In one end of it is a hall, in the other a store which has been intermittently occupied. It is now a billiard and pool room. The hall is the present place of many festivities.

Mr. William Gollin is one of the business men of the place. He owns a small, gasoline powered sawmill, and also a store in which fishing tackle, candy and fruit are for sale. Mr. Charles Bradford is the owner of a portable sawmill.

In the winter the village is a quiet place. The men are away cutting wood, a number of extra duties fall upon the women and money is none too plentiful. In the spring, summer and fall, however, there is a revivification. The men return to their homes, put by their axes and take out and prepare their canoes. In April the first sportsmen arrive. A little later a moving picture show begins its annual visits. Two or three times a week it comes to the village

LATER DAYS IN THE VILLAGE

and is said to take away weekly fifty dollars. These shows are interesting occasions when village folk and visitors assemble like one large family. The children gather in animated groups well to the front, often sitting on the floor in a great circle between the settees and curtain. A wide mantlepiece over the fireplace in the rear of the hall is usually occupied by several small boys. Bags of peanuts are freely passed around, and everybody has a good time. Frequent dances are given in this hall in the spring and early summer. Lady Washington's reel, Money Musk, Virginia reel and Portland fancy are still favorites here. The new dances however are not neglected.

Fourths of July, in the last few years, have been celebrated in the old fashioned manner. Water sports take place in the morning, foot races and novel contests of various sorts in the early afternoon. A ball game concludes the afternoon sports. There is dancing in the hall from an early hour in the afternoon until late at night. Ice Cream and other refreshments are for sale. Balloon men are in attendance with their gay colored wares. Fire crackers and pistols constantly pop. Automobile parties from the nearest towns come to the village, and, if the day is pleasant, there is ceaseless animation.

A ball team was organized in the summer of 1920. Many Saturday afternoons during the summer have been enlivened by ball games. The team has been successful in its contests with neighboring teams.

The Grand Lake Stream Company, Mr. Herbert Bacon and Mr. Everett Campbell own small excursion steamers. These, of course, are primarily for the use of sportsmen and summer guests, but the village folk occasionally have fishing and picnic trips in them. A number of guides and summer residents have motor boats, and nearly every man in the Plantation has at least one canoe. The "Robert H.", named for and for a long time owned by Mr. Robert Southerland, is a large, stern wheel, freight boat of the same type as the Company's boats, the "H. L. Drake" and the "Fanny Bates." In 1919 this boat was purchased by the Eastern

Pulpwood Company, rebuilt and renamed "Eastern." It is principally used in the spring and early summer to tow logs.

Now and then young people have gone away from Grand Lake Stream and acquired distinction or eminence elsewhere. Martin Butler was one of the first of these. After the accident in the tannery which cost him his right arm, he learned to write with his left hand. He became the publisher of "Butler's Journal," a weekly paper of Frederickton, New Brunswick. Fred Calligan, son of Mr. and Mrs. Thomas Calligan, has become a successful ranch owner in Washington State.

It is to the people who spend their lives here that the strongest interest is attached, however. They possess the sturdy traits of the first pioneers of America. The conditions of their lives make them self reliant and unaffected in manner. Shut away from the rest of the world all winter, save for the slender ties of more or less regular mail, they are ready with a hospitable welcome for returning friends or for strangers when the fishing, vacation and hunting season comes again. The resident guides of the village are:

Bacon, Elmer
Bacon, Herbert
Bagley, George
Bradford, Charles
Brown, Bernard
Brown, Earl
Brown, Edward
Brown, George
Brown, John
Brown, John V.
Brown, Seth
Brown, Truman
Brown, William
Campbell, Everett
Calligan, Charles
Chambers, Alexander

McArthur, George
McLoed, Fletcher
Moore, William
Kneeland, Harvey
Smith, Ernest
Smith, George
Smith, Zealous
Sprague, Charles
Sprague, Joseph
Sprague, Raymond
Sprague, Stephen
Sprague, Vernor
Sprague, William
Wheaton, Arthur
White, Charles
White, Charles C.

BALL'S CAMPS

FISHING FROM A PIER

Chambers, Angus
Chambers, Benjamin
Elsmore, Eben
Gollin, William
Gould, Hill
Gould, Frank
Hoar, Paul
Holmes, Arthur
Holmes, Frank
McArthur, Abraham
McArthur, Franklin

White, Fred
White, Horace
White, William
Whitehead, William
Woodward, Alonzo
Yates, Arthur
Yates, Eugene
Yates, Irving
Yates, Percy
Yates, Wallace

With two or three exceptions every family in the village is represented here at least once. The names show the English or Scotch ancestry of practically every family. In addition to the guides here mentioned there will usually be a few more, Indians, former residents, or residents of nearby places, who come to the village for the fishing season.

CHAPTER X

Grand Lake Stream in the World War

The village did its full share in the World War. One of the first to feel and respond to its call was Ernest Smith, son of Mrs. Alonzo Woodward and grandson of one of the pioneers of Township 21. He enlisted in the United States Navy in 1916 and was stationed on the U. S. S. "Kearsage".

Alexander Chambers, great grandson of Mary Ann Cass Hold, and great, great grandson of David Cass, the Township's first settler, enlisted in the Navy in March 1917. He was trained at the Naval station at Providence, R. I., and served on the ships "North Dakota," "Black Hawk," "New Mexico," and others. He was under Admiral Hugh Rodman and saw much active service in French and English as well as in American waters. He was mustered out of the service on the 18th of October, 1919.

Eldon Gould, son of Martha Yates Gould and the late Gorham Gould and grandson of the pioneers William Gould and Samuel Yates, enlisted in the Navy in May, 1917. He was sent to the Rhode Island training station and afterward faithfully served as fireman on the ship "New Jersey" for the duration of the war. He died of diphtheria while still in service on this ship in April, 1919.

Village boys to serve in the U. S. Army for the World War were:

Hill M. Gould   Infantry   Camp Devens
George M. McLoed (Corp.) Infantry Camp Devens
Zealous A. Smith   Infantry   Camp Devens
Ernest E. Sprague   Infantry   France
William E. Turner   Infantry   Camp Devens
Edward Arthur White   Engineers   France
Oliver White   Infantry   Portland, Me.

Ernest Sprague was mustered into service on May 28th, 1918. He was sent to Camp Devens. He volunteered for service in France and was sent abroad after less than

IN THE WORLD WAR

a month's training. He was a member of the 39th Infantry Regiment, Company A, 4th Division.

Edward Arthur White also volunteered for service in France. After four weeks training he was sent abroad. He was assigned to Company C, 504th Engineers and served with his company until the end of the war. Neither of these boys received wounds.

William Henry Medcalf, locally known as "Billy", early won distinction in the war. The village has only a partial claim to him, however. He lived here for several years when a small boy, then went with his parents to Dennysville. He later returned to the village and had been living here three years when the war broke out. He went at once to New Brunswick and enlisted in a Canadian regiment. He was sent to France early in 1915 and served continuously with a Canadian-Scottish unit until the end of the war—save for a few months when various wounds were healing in hospitals. He was several times recommended for gallantry in action. He has a Military Medal for risking his life to sit by a dying stranger in "no man's land" while shells were dropping around him, and machine guns were "beating their devil's tatoo." A bar, signifying additional citation for valor, was added to this medal. Later he received the Victoria Cross for "most conspicuous bravery, initiative and devotion to duty in attack."

The village subscribed $8,000 to various Liberty Loans, and $2,400 in War Saving Stamps. Contributions of over $200 were made to the Red Cross relief funds in addition to the cost of the large quantities of material used by the women in sewing and knitting for that Society.

CHAPTER XI

Description of the Village

"Just over the Maine border
  Some thirty miles or more
From where the St. Croix empties in
  At Calais' sea girt shore,
There stands amid the rock ribbed hills,
  Renowned for fish and game,
The little town my heart still thrills,
  The town without a name."

This verse is from a poem written by Martin Butler, called "The Town Without a Name." It is descriptive of the village. Yet the name Grand Lake Stream belongs to this spot as truly as its waters, its forests and its air belong to it. Since the days when an embryo village of sportsmen's tents rested periodically upon its uncultivated sods to the present days of civilized dwellings it has possessed it by natural endowment.

Shortly after the Plantation was organized the following description was sent to the Secretary of State at Augusta. "Description of Grand Lake Stream Plantation: Eight miles north and south, six miles east and west, bounded as follows: North by Talmage, east by Indian Township, south by Number 27, and Plantation 21, west by Number 6. The tannery and village are in the southwest corner at the foot of Grand lake. The road starts at the east side of the town and runs southwest across it to Number 6. There are a few farms situated on the road between Indian Township and the village."

The village occupies but a small part of this immense tract. The clearing, regardless of surveyor's plans, is about three quarters of a mile long and at the widest place one half mile wide. In all it contains about one half square mile of land. In addition to this open space there are the farms on the Milford and Princeton road. These are the

DESCRIPTION OF THE VILLAGE   83

Cass farms, the Hawkins farm, the farm called by the Shaw brothers the Poor Farm and the one cleared by the Rev. Moses Gardner.   West of the stream there are two small irregularly shaped fields.

The clearing is nearly oval in shape.   The dam stretches almost across its northern end. Beginning here in a tumultuous rush, as the water pours through the gate, the stream winds through the village in a narrow, shallow bed. The former ugly scar of the canal bank is now almost obliterated. Save for a short space just below the dam and another below the bridge the banks are well covered by trees and bushes.   The current of the stream is rapid, and the frequent rips sparkle in the sunshine, or in dull weather make enlivening bits of foam.   In summer the stream is a community bath tub—auxiliary to the lake. It sometimes serves the humble purpose of wash tub.   Many of the homes depend upon it for water for domestic purposes.   It is like a beneficent and dominating personality, a vital factor of village life.

Long, uneven ridges rise gently above both banks. On the sides of these ridges that slope toward the water most of the houses are built.   Most of them face it, their backs turned to the encircling forests.   The land is rocky and hilly, although the quality of the soil is good. Several springs bubble out on the hill sides and flow down to the stream. In summer some of these brooks become dry while in the spring they overflow their banks and make marshy places. From the dam, from some parts of the easterly ridge, from the knoll on which "Ouananiche Lodge" stands and from the road which straggles past it to "Tough End" the lake can be seen.   On a fair day it stretches broad and blue with a far, hazy border of trees and low mountains. On a dull day it is veiled in leaden mist and obscurity. Looking in the other direction from Water street, or from the Treadwell and Ball camps, the stream opens a gap for the broad, blue top of Harmon mountain, sixteen miles away, to show behind the trees. Looking upward the sky stretches unobscured in a vast arch. Its edges visibly curve downward far behind the ragged lines of trees that shut the village into the great forest.

In the winter much is changed. The evergreen trees show darker against the snow, and bare branches make an intricate brown mass, or stand out in fanciful relief from a white world. The sky seems lower: the roads are lined with snow banks, many paths branch out from them and lead to the houses. The lake is white with deep ice and snow. Even the stream is frozen save for a narrow space where the current is swift.

Several logging roads bore straggling, sometimes intersecting lines into the woods. In the fall when mosquitoes and black flies are gone these make pleasant walks. In the darker places are great beds of many varieties of ferns and in the less shaded spots are many wild flowers. Sumac blossoms, the red clusters of berries on the mountain ash trees, frost brightened blackberry vines and maple trees deck the forest greens. At this time too can be found beech nuts, the only nuts that are plentiful in the Plantation.

In the spring and early summer there are places where the ground is almost literally covered with violets. Later come the wild cherry blossoms, mountain laurel, wild carrot, daisies, goldenrod and a great variety of wild flowers. Wild strawberries are very abundant and so too are raspberries and blueberries. The trees are chiefly pine, hemlock, spruce, fir, cedar, birch and maple. In lesser number are the beeches, larches, alders, willows, oaks, and elms.

There are thickets by the stream from which come varied and beautiful bird songs. Song sparrows, bluebirds, catbirds, wood thrushes and the shy hermit thrush are all here and many more besides. Swallows wheel ceaselessly over the stream to catch the abundant flies. At night whippoorwills often call incessantly. At dusk night hawks fly about busily. In August there will be a regular visitation of fly catchers.

The air of the village is now clear and sweet. It frequently smells of pine trees, or the mingled odors of the

DESCRIPTION OF THE VILLAGE 85

many kinds of forest trees will permeate it, or sometimes, if the air is heavy, the pungent smell of burning wood comes down from the chimneys. One of the interesting features of the village is its wood piles. Every house has one, and some of them almost rival the house in size. Sometimes the woodpile is a stacked heap; sometimes it is a carefully arranged pile. They are seldom under cover. Upon them the inhabitants depend not only for cooking fires, but to keep the winter's cold out of the houses.

Two sorts of life mingle here, but are distinctly differentiated. A curious human mosaic is fitted snugly in the broad, green setting of the woods. Primitive America and the twentieth century are in actual contact. The women knit stockings and underwear at home, not only in war times but at all times for family needs. Here are the big catalogues of the famous mail order houses for an up to date market while the local stores carry groceries, paint, tinware, drygoods, boots and shoes and an incalculable number of other things. Here are primitive well sweeps, huge piles of sawed and split stove wood, and in the houses braided rugs, airtight stoves and water pails. Here are automobiles while the community's forty or more cows feed at will by the roadside or stray for miles into the forests. Through the narrow, dusty roads, or over Indian hill by the blueberry bushes, as the dusk falls, the cows come home driven by the tanned, often barefooted children. Cow bells tinkle discordantly, the voices of the children mingle with the gurgle of the rips, the low roar of the dam and the songs and twitter of birds. The small rural processions pass other little processions of sportsmen, returning from a day upon the lake, conducted by guides who bend under the weight of luncheon baskets, coats, cushions and sometimes of nets sagging with fish. So unaffectedly runs life, so outwardly peaceful is the village it is hard to realize that here, as elsewhere, falls the chastening, incorporeal rain that nurtures heart ache and discontent.

CHAPTER XII

Fish and Game

"Stretching from the Penobscot to the St. Croix, the boundary line between the United States and New Brunswick, and from the Atlantic ocean on the south to an almost unbroken wilderness on the north, Washington County is probably one of the finest fishing and hunting regions in this country."*

This is still true. Grand lake and its stream are home waters for the landlocked salmon, the fish which the Indians called ouananiche. For seventy seasons at least sportsmen have tussled here with these lively fish. It is said that in the days of Grover Cleveland the fame of them reached even to the White House and but for an unexpected stress of affairs the village would have been visited by him and Joseph Jefferson. Many distinguished fishermen have been attracted hither. From shortly after the ice leaves the lake in the spring until the end of June salmon rise with alacrity for the pretty, little artificial flies that are cast to them. Again in September their appetite for these dainties revives. These are, of course, the especially favorable times for taking them, but there is no day in the whole summer when by trolling on the lake with live bait they cannot be caught. In the stream are many pools where they lie concealed, but from which a skillfully thrown fly will lure them. Just above the dam fly fishing is also successful. In the proper season this is the place of greatest attraction in the village. As many fishermen will try their luck there as can find room on the piers. For each fisherman there will usually be a number of spectators. The interest and excitement of a "catch" never fail.

The ouananiche, or land locked salmon, are a handsome, silver colored, dark spotted fish. They are strong and fight hard when hooked. The female, it is said, has the most beautiful and symmetrical contours of all fish. Salmon in

*New York Tribune, August 27th, 1900.

THE STREAM and SECOND HATCHERY. Taken about 1887

Grand lake or the stream seldom weigh more than seven pounds, although in the summer of 1920 an eight and three-quarters pounds salmon was landed. The usual size of those caught is two or three pounds. It is estimated that sportsmen stopping in the village and the home fishermen together annually take about ten thousand of them. The lake is freshly stocked every year so that the supply never runs out.

Next to the salmon the togue rank in favor. They are lake trout, and grow very large. A fish weighing thirty-two pounds has been landed according to the "Washington County Railroad Magazine." During this summer (1920) a nineteen pounds togue was actually landed. These fish, however, are rare exceptions to the rule. An eight or ten pounds togue is an excellent fish to catch, and larger than the average. Togue, unlike salmon, make no desperate fight for life. They will lie on the bottom of the lake and resist by their weight the pull of the line. They are often caught in the winter through holes cut in the sometimes three feet thick ice. Occasionally a salmon is pulled through these holes, but this is a difficult feat. Other edible fish in the lake are white perch, pickerel (which are often caught for the market) and a little, delicious fish, weighing from a pound to a pound and a half and called white fish. White fish have such tender mouths that a hook will tear out, but they are caught in great numbers in nets.

"Sometimes," said a guide, "as many as seven hundred are taken in one net in a single night."

They are caught in the spring and fall. A net, finely meshed and long, is stretched near the shore in a favorable place. The bottom of it is weighted with lead, and the top buoyed with cork. When the fish try to swim through it to the shallow water for food their fins are caught in the meshes of the net, and they are hopelessly entangled. Of course no "sport" indulges in this method of fishing, but for the home fisherman who wishes to stock his larder it is most efficacious. When lightly smoked white fish keep for a long time.

Some of the most successful fishers are hawks. These powerful birds fly over the stream in long, sweeping curves. Sometimes they hang suspended in the air, scanning the water, then suddenly swoop down, make a great splash and rise with a wriggling fish clutched in their claws.

Years ago, before the Washington County railroad was built, and the Princeton and Calais railroad had no connections to make with other trains, the leisure of the woods often infected the engineer and conductor of the latter road. *They carried guns, and as they puffed along kept a lookout for game. If any was sighted the train stopped and a shot was taken. Once, so runs the legend, the conductor of the train shot and wounded a buck deer. The frightened animal ran back along the track for several rods before it succumbed and fell over the embankment. The excited spectators, passengers who had left the train to see the sport, hurried on board again, the engine was reversed and the train backed to the spot. The deer was hoisted on board and the train resumed its way to Princeton with everybody on it satisfied.

No stops of this sort are now made, but deer are still plentiful in the whole region. So also are moose. In the fall a moose call given on the shore of Grand lake will seldom fail to bring one or two of these big creatures into sight.

The woods that are many miles deep on all sides of the village, save for the short open space of lake boundary, are still primitive although the trees are of the young generations that follow the woodman's axe. The decay and litter of ages are here. So too are mossy boulders, hills and hummocks, deep crevasses between frost riven rocks, brooks, trickling springs, deep shadowed thickets, dens of black bears and homes and haunts of hundreds of other wild animals.

All the gear of savagry, save only the wild Indians, remains. Even Mystery has left her eerie footprints on the leaf mold and moss for there is an "Injun devil"—long, gray, lithe, panther like—who lurks in the deep shadows,

*Washington County Railroad Magazine.

FISH AND GAME

Sometimes his blood curdling cry falls upon the ears of lonely campers, or of children strayed too far from the village; sometimes his pursuing shadow is seen on the lonely, night shaded roads of the region. He is doubtful game for the hunter, but the black bears are still so numerous that the state pays a bounty of five dollars for every one killed. They leave their dens by the end of March, or the first of April. Sometimes they are seen on the roads at a little distance from the village; sometimes a glimpse may be caught of one swimming in the lake. Few are captured by shooting. Trapping is the most successful way of taking them. A favorite method is to conceal a powerful steel trap in a slightly hollowed place beneath fallen branches and leaves. An appetizing morsel is tied on a branch over it. In attempting to reach the bait the bear falls through the rubbish that conceals the trap, and is caught in its jaws. To make his capture doubly sure the ground around the trap is sometimes pegged with pointed sticks. Directly over the trap will be the only soft spot on which to stand, and he will pick his way to it. Another and more primitive way of trapping bears which entails no outlay of money, but requires considerable work and ingenuity, is by the use of dead poles. This is the method the pioneer David Cass used. In taking the bait placed for him the bear liberates a heavy log which is suspended over it. It falls upon him, and breaks his back. Lately it has been discovered that spoiled oranges are a toothsome dainty which he cannot resist. Phosphorus also has great attractions for him. After the first of June bear skins are not good so the trapping is done in the early spring.

The lesser animals found in these woods and valuable for their fur are weasel (whose skin sells for ermine), Canadian lynx and Bay lynx, muskrat, mink, otter, red and gray 'fox, (the latter rather rare), black or fisher cat and rabbit.

It is estimated that at least five hundred dollars worth of furs are sold from the village yearly. These are in addition to furs carried from here to Princeton whose annual output they help to swell to a value of nearly three thousand dollars.

Big lake is one of the best places for duck and bird shooting in New England. Partridge, woodcock, black duck, pintail, green and blue winged teal, blue bill and simp are abundant in the lake. In the marshes are long legged blue heron and a few coot and rail. The presence of the latter bird is not generally known.

Many ducks are also found on the inlets of Grand lake. Loons and sheldrakes are very common there.

CHAPTER XIII
The Hatchery

The first fish cultural work in Grand Lake Stream was begun in 1868. At that time the Commissioners of Fisheries of both Maine and Massachusetts conjointly collected a quantity of eggs of land locked salmon, or ouananiche. They matured them at a place in the woods half a mile or so west of the stream where there is a spring. For three years work was done here without protection of any sort from the weather. In 1871 a rough log building was erected over the spring. In the next year the United States Commissioner took over the care of the work. For some years this station was a sub-station of the Craig Brook Hatchery. Mr. Charles G. Atkins was in charge of the latter place, and under him William Munson was fish culturist in charge here. Mr. Munson, it is interesting to note, was a nephew of the Ananijah Munson who lived by the stream for a few years in the Township's early days.

Most painstaking work was done in the log building, although Mr. Atkins' report of it published in the "Report of the United States Fish Commissioner" says: "The site of the hatchery house is a very unfavorable one. Both spring and brook water can be used, but the brook is a tiny one, and in cold and dry weather shrinks to a very insignificant volume, while the spring issues from the ground at such an elevation from the swamp through which it flows, that at best we can barely get our troughs high enough to avoid flooding by freshets. Thus is there no opportunity of aerating the water by a fall, and the troughs must be placed upon a level with the floor, an unfavorable position for work....No larger spring could be found in the neighborhood, there was no clean and ample brook, and the water of Grand lake stream itself, though probably unsurpassed for such a purpose by any in the world, could not be used on account of certain physical difficulties which I saw no way of surmounting with the means at my disposal."

It was attempted to care for two million eggs at this small place. The work was well done and surprisingly successful, although owing to lack of room and proper conveniences many of the eggs were insufficiently nourished. "It was", says the report of Mr. Atkins in 1877, "finally decided to put in a temporary hatchery house on the west bank of the stream at the first fall below the dam. Even here we had a fall of but little more than ten feet and liability to flooding by spring freshets.... The new hatchery house was a humble structure, only twenty feet by ten, but there was placed in it three troughs, each seventeen inches deep, which had an aggregate capacity of nearly a million eggs. Wire trays were employed about twelve inches square, nested in frames carrying twenty trays per frame—the identical apparatus used at this establishment in 1875 and yearly since. The water was taken from the open stream through a covered plank conduct."

The new hatchery was supplementary to the old one. It was experimental, but the success of it warranted the erection of a permanent structure by the stream in 1879. The new building was eighteen feet by twenty-two. It stood very near the spot now occupied by the summer camp of the late Professor J. W. White. It was used only to bring part of the eggs through their earlier stages of development. At this same time efforts were also made to increase the supply of water at the old hatchery in the woods. Yet together these buildings proved inadequate for the work it was desired to accomplish. In December, 1880, a structure, designed as an addition to the first two buildings, was hastily erected in a small cove on the west side of the lake just above the dam. By another year the new building seemed so well located that it was enlarged. It was built upon the side of a steep incline, and had "six floors arranged in a descending series with a floor space in all of fifteen hundred feet," says Mr. Atkins' report. The floors were cemented, and the stone foundation walls were from one to eighteen feet high. Mr. Atkins says of it: "The location of this hatchery is an exceedingly favorable

THE HATCHERY 93

one, and it is a matter of regret that the facilities existing at this point were not discovered at the institution of the establishment. The ground was, in its original condition, heavily strewn with boulders, large and small, and beneath them were interstices through which the water of the spring stole away in such measure as to give the impression that the supply was not only small but inconstant. It was only after the tangled maze of shrubs was torn away and part of the surface earth removed that the permanent character of the spring could be observed."

Besides the expected plentiful supply of water there were other advantages of the new station. Mr. Atkins further says: "I make no doubt that all the serious losses which during the earlier years occasionally befell the stocks of eggs in development and transportation might have been avoided had we then possessed the facilities of Hatchery Number Three. Among the minor disadvantages which we might have escaped may be mentioned the labor and risk of carrying the eggs by hand from the fishing grounds over a half mile of rough road, often by night, the difficulty of guarding well the property so far out of sight and hearing, and the many weary days spent by Mr. Munson in the transfer of the young fish from the house to the stream in the month of June amid tormenting clouds of mosquitoes and black flies. This will henceforth be the headquarters for the establishment. Here the eggs will be packed for shipment, and the reserve hatched."

These headquarters, when completed, comprised a superintendent's cottage, a small ice house and a woodshed as well as the main hatchery. It was originally intended to buy the land on which these buildings stood. An option was secured, but at this juncture the final collapse of the tannery occurred. There was some confusion in the subsequent sale of the village property which had belonged to the Company (of which this site was a part). The Grand Lake Stream Company became the owner of it. The buildings passed with the land to the new owners, and in consequence of this miscarriage of its plans the Government now pays a yearly rental for the use of the premises.

Work was suspended in this hatchery from 1892 to 1897. In the latter year needed repairs were made and work resumed. By that time it had been discovered that the sanguine hopes of an adequate water supply were badly founded. The spring proved to be inconstant. A new site was finally selected almost where the Company's sawmill once stood. A dam was put across the end of the canal there, and an unstinted stream flows over it and through a wooden conduct to the troughs where the fingerlings are kept. This hatchery was begun on Sept. 12th, 1906, and has since been used with success, although the building is small.

Eggs are taken in November. The work lasts about three weeks. The report of 1877 gives 2,159,000 as the number obtained in that year. Of these 470,000 were hatched for Grand lake. The rest were shipped to other places in the country. In 1887 there were taken 865,834 eggs, and 208,000 were hatched for the lake. In 1897 the number of eggs taken was 289,662. 114,171 fry were hatched from these for this lake. These were retained in the hatchery until they were fingerlings before they were liberated. In 1907 there were taken 610,000 eggs and 59,740 were retained for this lake. A slight idea of the work of the station is thus obtained by these figures for one year in each of several successive decades. In 1900 there were 33,862 fingerlings liberated in the lake. This is the smallest contribution ever made from the hatchery to the lake. The largest was in 1902 when 429,765 fry and 58,835 fingerlings were liberated.

In the later part of April the eggs—probably from eighty to eighty-five per cent. of the whole number—hatch. The spawn are in condition for shipment in February. They are packed in cases of dry moss, and usually arrive at their destination in good condition. The fry grow to be fingerlings in about four months. They are put in the lake in the October following the April in which they are hatched.

In some of the earlier years the hatchery was supported

THE HATCHERY

by contributions from the United States Government, and from a few individual states. Thus in 1877 the United States gave $1,400, Massachusetts $500, Connecticut $300, and New Hampshire $200. Each contributor received a proportionate ratio of the eggs, after twenty-five per cent. had been reserved for Grand lake. In some years Maine was a contributor to the maintenance fund; in some New Hampshire and Connecticut did not contribute. In later years the United States Government has borne the entire expense of the hatchery. The station has been placed under the charge of the Green Lake hatchery.

Since 1912 thirty-five per cent. of the eggs taken have been reserved for this lake. The other sixty-five per cent. of eggs are given by the United States to applicants whose requests are considered worthy. Since the establishment of the hatchery here eggs from it have been shipped to various lakes and ponds in the middle west and to places in the more northerly of the southern states. They have also been sent hence to France, Germany, England, Japan and other countries. They make these long journeys without serious injury, and are then successfully hatched.

It is said that some time ago a United States Army officer who had fished in this lake visited Japen. A fishing expedition was arranged for part of his entertainment there. He landed a fish whose plucky fight and appearance seemed familiar.

"It's a land locked salmon from Grand Lake Stream, Maine," explained the Japanese official who accompanied him.

The hatchery has been especially fortunate in the men selected to care for it. They have all been not only good fish culturists, but well liked residents of the village. Some of them have lived here several years. Mr. William Munson remained in charge until about 1904. William Drummy of the Green Lake hatchery then took his place and remained here until October of the next year. Mr. W. O. Buck was the next culturist in charge, remaining until 1909. He came here from the Craig Brook station. Mr. John A.

Story, also of Craig Brook took his place, beginning his duties in November 1909. He was transferred to the Green Lake hatchery in the spring of 1906. Mr. Frederick Foster of the Saratoga, (Wyoming) hatchery succeeded him and in February 1919 was himself succeeded by Mr. Story who was returned from the Green Lake hatchery.

Mr. Wallace W. Yates began work as assistant in 1904 and has rendered most valuable service since that time. Mr. Yates is a nephew of the pioneer Samuel Yates.

CHAPTER XIV
Later Indians

The pressure of white settlers slowly restricted the Indians until by 1866 the remnants of the Passamaquoddy tribe had nearly all been gathered in two settlements—one at Pleasant Point on the bay, and the other at Peter Dana's Point on Big lake. Parties of these Indians still make the annual migrations up into the Grand lake neighborhood. They usually come soon after the ice leaves the lake in the spring. A favorite camp site is the slope facing the stream on the eastern ridge, and in the northern end of the village. This spot is called Indian hill and on it is a little portable house given to the Indians some years ago by a visiting sportsman. Some of the Indians paddle up the lake a little way and camp on its eastern bank. Formerly they stayed in these camps the whole summer long. More recently their visits have lasted but a few weeks in the spring.

Squaws, in the earlier days of the village, used to wear a skirt and a loose sack. The skirt was made of three widths of cloth sewed up straight and gathered at the waist. When one of them acquired anything new it was put on over these garments. Nothing was discarded until it dropped off. In course of time some of the squaws were incased in many layers of clothes—none of them undergarments. The latter were not an Indian fashion. No matter what the weather they always added to their costumes a heavy woolen shawl. It was folded cornerwise and the tip trailed on the ground behind them. A red cotton handkerchief tied over the head was the last and picturesque touch to the toilet.

The men wore any old clothes they could get and as many as fortune allotted them. They would make excursions into the woods to gather materials to manufacture paddles, tables of alder fancifully twisted and topped with birch bark, small boxes of birch bark—prized by housewives as receptacles for salt, soda, spices, coffee, tea and other things— and baskets. In the earlier village days their baskets were usually coarse and heavy, such as clothes, market and bushel baskets. At that time they were often swapped for provisions. A clothes basket would be exchanged for a peck of potatoes, a fair sized basket given even for a cup of sugar. Later they learned to color their splints and to make more fanciful and lighter sorts, and also to make the beautiful sweet grass baskets. Before canvas canoes came into use all those used on the lake were Indian birch bark canoes. They were made of a single flawless piece of bark. It was often a day's search in the mosquito and black fly infested forests to find such a piece. Articles manufactured here were taken as far as Calais and Eastport in search of customers.

The Indians are now much better clothed than formerly, and this is largely due to the better prices that their baskets bring. Each of them receives two annual dividends from the state which together amount to about a dollar and a half. The state maintains schools at each point, looks after the poor, pays a bounty on all crops raised and otherwise assists them. These Indians have been Catholics since the days of the Jesuit Missions in Nova Scotia, New Brunswick and at the mouth of the Penobscot river. Some of those who know them best, however, think that they still have a lingering faith in the old manitous. When Klooscup, the first man and master of all things, was deprived of his high estate by the Jesuits the old Indians said and believed that he retired to an island in the far north. He is still there, making a great number of bows and arrows with which the white people are sometime all to be destroyed. Then the Indians will again own the earth, and all will be as it was. *The Passamaquoddies, more than any other group of the Abenaki family, have retained early traditions and legends.

Peter Dana, for whom the point on Big lake was named, was governor of this branch of the tribe about seventy-five

---

*Sylvester, in his "Indian Wars of New England" makes this statement. The meaning of Abenaki is said to be The People of the Morning, or of the First Light.

LATER INDIANS

years ago. He is remembered as a powerful man of unusual wisdom. Captain Lewey, another chief, and for whom Lewey lake was named, was also a notable member of the tribe. He is said to have been the first settler of Princeton which for a long time was called Lewey's Island. He was a tall, stalwart man with features typically Indian, and he and his sons were very proud of their undiluted Indian blood. He was enterprising and in an age and vicinity when much drinking was the rule reasonably sober. At times he was a lumber contractor, and sometimes he acted as boss of a gang of river drivers. In the latter capacity he worked for a dollar and a half a day while the men under him were paid two dollars. When he was asked how this happened he said it was worth a half a dollar a day to be boss. He was very honest. To prove that he could borrow money without security he did, one morning, borrow from a bank where he was known, two hundred dollars without security. He carried it in his pocket, frequently taking it out to display it, until just before the bank closed when he deposited it. These are but two of the stories told of him.

His son Athien is also favorably remembered. He farmed and guided and when he died, August 31st, 1899, he had a substantial bank account.

Another of the notable governors was Joe Pierpole. The following story is told of him: Government officials were visiting the point when one of them asked him to name three wishes.

"By jolly," said he after some reflection, "I wish Big lake all rum!"

"What next?" he was asked.

The old fellow scratched his head. "Have St. Croix river all rum too," he answered triumphantly at last.

"And last, Capt'n?"

This required still more cogitation, but at length his mouth distended in a seraphic smile.

"Have more rum," he said.

He often came to Grand lake and acted as guide to visiting sportsmen. Other Indians to act as guides in former days were John Newel, Nicholas Lola and two brothers called after the Indian fashion Tomah Joe and Gabriel Tomah. These guides were sometimes great story tellers. Gabriel Tomah was especially gifted in the art. Two of his stories and others of more or less local interest are in the appendix of this book.

CHAPTER XV
The Sewing Circles and the Church

The history of the village sewing circle seems like an irregular flow and ebb of tide. Sometimes its activity has been very high; sometimes it had fallen very low indeed. It has never ceased to exist, however. The responsibility of earning a part of the minister's salary has kept it alive, but it has taken other and more especial objects to arouse it into great endeavor. Sometimes it has been divided into two circles, each with bylaws and a name. Nevertheless the same devoted women have worked for unselfish ends however they were named, or divided. The only real change has been when daughters have taken the place of mothers whom age, ill health or death have retired from its roll of workers, or when an occasional new comer in the village has taken a place in it. Since the settlement of the village the women have pushed to completion many enterprises. They raised money to build the cupola on the school house, and to buy and hang the bell in it. They also paid for a fence around the old cemetery, and they bought a carpet for the platform in the school house hall. All of these things have been accomplished by selling the work of their needles, and by the proceeds of periodical suppers. At length it was determined to undertake the really valorous project of building a church. Perhaps it will be remembered that the first religious services were held in the log school house where Mrs. Sprague taught. After the Shaw brothers built the frame school house services were held there. The school house had always been used for a great variety of secular purposes. Lodge meetings, dances, town meetings and nearly every sort of social gathering were held in the hall under its hospitable roof. A growing discontent that it should be the only place in the village for religious services culminated in this resolve of the women that a church should be built. To many residents of the village there had often come visions of a church which should stand in their midst, a token of their reverence, an inspiration for good lives and service. It was the women who at last had the courage and force to transmute the vision into a reality, aided, however, most generously by many of the men.

The circle was suffering one of its periodical divisions, and was lasping into semi-apathy when it was reanimated by the forming of plans for this accomplishment. Ten of the indomitable ones of both circles became the founders of a new circle which they called the "Church Benefit League." In a short time other members of the two partly disintegrated circles were attracted to it, and an unusually plucky campaign to raise money was begun. The League naturally encountered some opposition, much scoffing and skepticism, but nothing discouraged its members and helpers. Inspired by the energy and zeal of Mrs. Lucinda Sprague, Mrs. Hannah Holmes, Mrs. Evie Moore and many others the women gave weekly suppers at the homes of different members of the League; they made and sold aprons, dresses, shirtwaists, patchwork quilts, braided rugs, knitted socks, mittens, gloves and underwear, and some of the women, after helping at all of these things and looking after their own households as well, found time to scrub. The school house was cleaned from top to bottom; the store where the dirt of the old tannery days still darkened the wood, was treated to rejuvenating applications of soap and water, and the dirt of carpenters, masons and other workmen was cleaned from a new camp. All of the money earned in these ways was turned into the church fund. These gifts of time and strength which busy wives and mothers gave to do this work should count greatly in the total of gifts that eventually paid for the church.

The weekly suppers netted the League from ten to fifteen dollars each. Sometimes a supper was given in the school house hall. For these occasions beans were baked in the ground in the old fashioned way. A Fourth of July dinner given out of doors netted them fifty dollars. A patchwork quilt in which each woman wrote her name in the square which she made was sold by ten cent tickets and

THE CHURCH

THE SEWING CIRCLE, THE CHURCH 103

brought in thirty dollars. Thus little by little the funds grew, and belief in the project grew also. Subscription papers were taken around. Nearly everybody in the Plantation was ready and willing to give. Still a few scoffers remained.

"De money, it is not in town. You have not enough to de nails buy," said one of these, called Little Pete, the Dane. "But," he added, to emphasize his disbelief, "you build de church, and I will de pulpit buy." The promise was not kept.

The League raised $1,635.90 by the sheer force of the practical genius of its members. The Congregational Building Society of New York lent an additional sum which enabled the village to have its church. Several generous donations and gifts helped to complete it.

The "Minute Book" of the church records that on March 29th, 1904, "the plan to build a church took root." This was shortly after the collapse of the tannery, and in perhaps the most discouraging period in the village's history. Therefore the League's achievement is especially noteworthy. On July 11th, four months after the work of raising money was begun, the sod was broken for the building, and two days later the church was organized. On July 17th, the cornerstone was laid, and on September 18th, of the same year (1904) services were held in the unfinished building. On Christmas day Sunday school was held in the finished vestry. The building was completed in the following September. Its approximate cost was two thousand dollars. It is called the Union Congregational Church.

Ministers in the village have almost without exception been theological students and engaged for the summer only. Usually there has been a different minister each summer. In the earlier days a few of these student ministers were boarded around. Latterly the parish, which is practically the whole village, has paid their board at some private house, or at the Grand Lake Hotel. In the winter religious services consist of Sunday school and Christian Endeavor meetings.

By continued effort the women have helped to pay the running expenses of the church. Shortly after its organization a society of children called "The Busy Bees" earned money in many ways for it, and helped materially toward the purchase of its first organ. Later another organ was earned by "The Drama Club." This club went to Princeton, Topsfield and Alexander to give plays in order to raise money for this gift to the church.

. . . .

Yet another high tide in the circle's life rose in 1914. This was when the project of a woman's building arose. The work of the circle had always been made difficult by the lack of a sufficiently large and convenient meeting place. The attendance at the fortnightly suppers held in the too small dining rooms of members was becoming slender. There was no good place for the sale of aprons and other needle products. The school hall, now converted into a high school, was no longer available for these purposes. Various expedients had been suggested, but to all of them there were serious objections. At length a few of the more energetic of the women resolved to have a building for themselves. The old circle was reformed and named "Old Fashioned Sewing Circle." A meeting was held at the home of Mrs. Ruth Wheaton with twenty-five members present. Mrs. Wheaton was elected president, and became at once the leader in an energetic campaign to raise money for a Circle Hall. A new round of suppers was given for ten and fifteen cents a plate, more aprons and children's garments were made, knitting done. Holiday and other sales of home made candy, cake and ice cream were undertaken. A small building fund was thus obtained. Of course the circle regularly contributed from its earnings to the salary of the minister, and to other church expenses. After two years of endeavor the women had accumulated $295 for their building. Like the women who pushed through the church project they met much opposition. It was even greater, in proportion to the undertaking, than that which had met the earlier and larger project. Nothing

THE SEWING CIRCLE, THE CHURCH

turned the "Old Fashioned Circle" from its purpose, however. Interested persons and visitors to the village contributed sums varying from ten to one hundred dollars. Mr. Webber gave them permission to cut five thousand feet of lumber from his woodland, and the St. Croix Paper Company of Woodland gave them a rent free lease of land upon which to erect the building.

The hall was built in the fall of 1916. It is a plain, one story and a half structure, but comfortable and large enough for all circle activities. It is homelike and cozy and furnished with the essentials for circle work, although its owners hope to add something to its finish and its conveniences. It was opened and a supper and a sale held on Christmas eve, 1916. Mr. Robert Black, theological student who served as minister during the summer of 1917, contributed, during that summer, the labor of putting two coats of paint on the outside of the building.

A branch of the Red Cross Society was formed in 1917, chiefly from circle members. All possible time was given to knitting and other war work, and so the finishing touches the women intend to give their building have been postponed.

CHAPTER XVI
Witteguergangum

Little of Witteguergaugum, or Grand lake, lies in the Plantation of Grand Lake Stream. Its southeastern extremity and Dyer cove are here, but the vast body of the lake lies in Township 6. The lake is, however, the natural completion of the village. It is to it as the door yard and garden are to a house. It is a source of recreation and of profit. The village, inclosed in a narrow space by the green walls of deep forests, would seem cramped without this wide, opened space beyond its tapered northern end. While more of Big lake than of Grand lake lies in the Plantation the former is too far away from the village to be in any sense a part of it.

Grand lake is twelve miles long and from four to ten miles wide. The government has never surveyed it, but many soundings have been taken by guides. Its depths have in this way been estimated to be in places two hundred feet and even more. The water is clear and exceptionally pure. Farm, Whitney and Dyer coves are broad arms which stretch to the south, north and east respectively. Many smaller coves dent the shores between them. Farm cove mountain, the low range called Whitney cove mountains and Pineo mountains make a pretty, irregular sky line which begins to the southwest and extends across the north and well to the east. These hills are variously estimated to be from three to five hundred feet in height. Despite the work of wood cutters they are covered with a thick growth of trees. The dark color of pines, spruce and hemlocks made eccentric shaped spots on the more plentiful deciduous trees, or raise grotesque tops above them to be silhouetted against the slope of the sky. The shores also are all thickly wooded although here and there a narrow opening marks the site of an old logging road, or the winter homes of wood cutters. Sometimes deer, moose and even bears are seen in the openings. The few summer camps of sportsmen show so indistinctly through the trees that the shores have a lonely, uninhabited look.

In 1905 the St. Croix Paper Company of Woodland obtained a right to flood the lake. The water is now seven feet or more higher than its natural level. Some of the natural beauties have, in consequence, been lost. Sandy beaches are covered; many trees at the water's edge are dead. The latter are now a fast disappearing fringe of gray, lifeless trunks and branches, some leaning, some still standing erect. They are phantom trees in the gray light of fog or storm, unsightly litter in sunshine. Presently, however, they will all have been swept away in the current, and perhaps new beaches will form.

More serious than these devastations are the slightly submerged islands On some of them clumps of dying trees still stand or lean, on others a few rocks or stumps rise above the water and on others there is no mark. These shallow places are well known, however, and no serious accidents have occurred no matter how dark or foggy it may have been. There are many islands that are not submerged. Bear island is the largest of these, and the next largest is Marks' island (named for Colonel Marks who bought the Township from Judge Hinckley). The third largest island is Hardwood.

The lake seems to be a bed of tumbled rock wreckage. Heaps of broken, water worn rocks rise in jagged peaks above the water, usually near the shore, but sometimes far out in the lake. Immense ledges line some of the shores, and great boulders jut out from the trees and bushes. Hoary and grim one boulder rises out of the water a hundred or more yards from the shore and well up on the western side of the lake. It is called Caribou rock because many years ago the pioneer, William Gould, is said to have seen a caribou upon it. It has a sullen, crouching attitude as if waiting for some great chance while the pageants of thousands of years pass before it. Perhaps it is a drift boulder, and came down from the north in a slow glacial procession, or it may have slipped from a neighboring hill long before even the Indians were here. Gulls lay their eggs in the slight hallows of its passive back and leave them there for the sun to hatch in often misplaced confidence in eagles, owls and hawks.

The pretty, fresh water gulls wheel and circle over the lake, or alight on the rocks where they look strangely large. Loons swim about in the water, or lift inquisitive heads to stare at passing boats. Occasionally they make their queer, wild, soprano cry. All summer long flocks of sheldrakes frequent the lake. It is an amusing thing to see them hurry in front of a motor boat without having the wit to swim to one side of its path.

On a summer afternoon the lake is all glittering blue color. Off to the north and west the shores are a hazy, luminous blue. The southern shores slightly take the tint from the sky and water and melt their deep green into the blue lake world. The lake is so large that steamers, motor boats and canoes scarcely disturb its solitude. Usually a few white clouds ride lazily across the sky, or mass over the tops of the trees near the horizon. Often the breeze will stir the tops of the waves into responsive white flecks. Thunder showers usually come down across the lakes to the village. The lightning can be seen streaking the sky, or darting down into the tree tops, but the thunder is moderate. The hills are too low for long reverberations.

The Plantation leases from the Grand Lake Stream Company landing privileges on the easterly side of the lake above the dam. It was here that the Company built its wharf. It gradually fell into a state of dilapidation. A row of boat houses rose upon some of its foundations. Attempts at repairs, sufficient to prevent accidents, were made occasionally by guides. At length, however, so little was left of it that the Plantation raised $800 dollars to build a new wharf. Stone foundations were laid and a plank floor laid over them. So swift is the current and so violent the action of the ice in the spring that frequent repairs are necessary.

Besides the boat houses near the wharf directly opposite

it on the western shore are more boat houses, another landing privilege and the third hatchery. The thick woods adjoin these thin ends of the village. Above the dam the lake is very narrow. Properly this is a part of the stream. It broadens gradually for about a mile, and then expands into the lake.

There is a legend which says that an Indian family once lived near Farm cove mountain. It was after the French Jesuits had led the Indians into the safe folds of the Catholic church. The head of the family was a zealous convert. One beautiful Sunday morning two members of his family wished to paddle on the still, shining lake. They were forbidden the pleasure. It was a holy day, said the father, and therefore wicked to paddle on the lake, but his children refused to obey him. So the Great Spirit punished them. He changed their bodies into swans, and sentenced their spirits to paddle each night forever on the lake. It is said they have been seen by lumbermen—two white figures in a white canoe paddling around and around an island near the cove.

The End.

The following poem was written by Mr. Orington Brown of Princeton who has called himself the "Burnt Land Poet."

Old Musquash Bridge

I was thinking today of the grand old way
    And my heart was lonely and sad;
But I'll give to the wind all sorrow, and sing
    A song that will make you glad.

I will cast on the air all sorrow and care
    And sing you a different lay.
I'll tell, if old Musquash bridge could speak,
    What the old wooden span would say.

If old Musquash bridge could speak
    It would tell of the olden days,
Way back in the year of seventy one
    From then to the present days.

If that old wooden bridge could speak
    It would tell of many a sail,
Of many a wild and stormy night,
    Of wind, and rain, and hail!

It would tell of many a pleasant sound
    In the days of early fall
When the feathered songsters flocked around—
The bark of the fox and the rabbit's bound,
    And the heron's distant call.

It would tell of the deafening roar
    Of the old muzzle loader's song,
Of the eagle's scream, of the valley's roar—
How the echoes rolled from shore to shore
    To the mouth of the Amazon.

It would tell how in the morning dew
  Fell the Injun's stealthy dips,
As he glided on in his light canoe,
With the bluffs of Cold spring full in view,
  To the mouth of old Flipper creek.

It would tell of the honk of the goose
  Above in the clear, blue sky,
And the midnight tread of the brindle moose
As he roams about on a forest cruise,
  And feeds in the rushes nigh.

It would tell how from the willows near
Comes the poacher's rifle crack—
The bleat and bound of the stricken deer,
As he falls on the bank in the rushes near
  With a bullet in his back.

It would tell how his life blood ebbs away
  And how, when the wardens come
And cruise the river up and down,
Not a trace of the poachers found—
  Not a sight of man or gun.

It would tell of the autos' rush and yell
  That make its old timbers squeak.
Ten thousand things it would tell to you,
Things that are old and things that are new,
  If that old wooden bridge could speak.

A Briton's Lonely Grave
by
S. Alonzo Day of Fairfield, Maine

Far away in the northern pine lands,
Those lands so like a dream,
A lonely grave is lying
By the banks of "Grand Lake Stream."
That grave is the grave of a Soldier boy
Who died long, long ago;
He served in the ranks of Old England
So the old Legends go.

Long years of more than a hundred
Have passed since that Autumn day
When a band of Britons made their camp
And prepared the night to stay;
Fain would they have gone farther
Ere that Autumn sun went down
But this comrad true was dying—
His life was nearly gone.

Worn out by the long, hard journey,
For they came from the distant sea,
And he'd held his place, as a Briton does,
In the ranks of his company.
Vain was the help they gave him
And plain could be seen that light—
That shines from the eyes of a dying soul—
When its spirit takes its flight.

By the silvery stream they laid him
While his spirit fought its way
From within its breaking prison
From its earthly house of clay.
'Twas then he called his comrads to him
And in a voice now hard to hear
He gave his farewell message
For the ones he loved so dear.

For them to carry back to England
When they sailed for that fair shore
To that home so dear now to him;
That old home he'd see no more.

Then he faltered for a moment,
With a trembling voice he said,
"Tenderly tell my dear old parents
For I know their hearts will break
As does a bow, when overburdened,
When they hear of my sad fate.
Tell them how I longed to see them
As death cooled my burning brow;
That death's journey would be brighter
Could I be with mother now.

"For I was taken from my old home
Taken by the King's command.
As a Soldier now I'm dying—
Dying in a foreign land."
Then his face grew strangely brighter
He was living far away
With his dear ones back in England
With a maiden fair and gay;
Strolling with her thro' that garden
Where the Hawthorne roses grew,
Just the same as on that evening
When he took his last adieu.

And his comrads as they listened,
Heard him chant a sweet refrain
With his lips now cold and lifeless,
Heard him speak his sweetheart's name,
As the Autumn slanting sunbeams
Brightened up the restless stream.
So her smiles gave to him glory
Glory in his final dream.
Thus he died this lad so tender,
Hardly had his life begun;
Thus he left his comrads weeping

Left them with the setting sun.
In that lonely grave they laid him
On that eve so long ago
While the trumpets softly sounded
And the muffled drums beat low.

By this grave you'll see no mourner
At Memorial time of year;
No thoughtful loving parent,
No one to shed a tear
Only a lonely Sumac tree
Now marks his place of rest;
As mother earth in her fond embrace
Now folds him to her breast.

Oh, Wanderer! As you pass this grave
'Tho' humble it may seem,
Do not esteem it lightly
For that simple mound doth screen
The dust of a worthy Hero,
A worthy Briton dead,
Where they laid him at rest so long ago
In his "Uniform of Red."
Awaiting the Resurrection Day
And on that morning bright
He will rise and perhaps forever
Wear a "Uniform of White."

The tradition here recounted was told Mr. Day's father by the Indians. It is supposed, although upon how truthful a tradition is impossible to determine, that the soldier was a drummer boy and that he died in a war that took place before the Revolution. The grave is about a half mile from the village on the east bank of the stream and is unmarked. A recent attempt to locate it was unsuccessful.

Another tradition, or surmise, ascribes this grave to a soldier who with others may have been sent from Nova Scotia, by way of these lakes and carries, to the assistance of Burgoyne near Saratoga, New York.

APPENDIX 115

Indian Names, Demons and Stories

On a surveyor's map, made before the beginning of the 19th century and preserved in the State House in Boston, Grand lake is called Witteguergaugum and Big lake Genesagenagun. Governor's point on an old document preserved there is called Nemcass point. In answer to a letter to the Bureau of American Ethnology at the Smithsonian Institution requesting information respecting these names the following has been received:

"The first, Genesagenagun (of which Genesagarumsis is another spelling), may probably mean pickerel lake.

"The second name, Witteguergaugum, may mean "Mill" lake or pond, seemingly referring to the existence of some kind of a mill at this point.

"The third may mean "fishery," if it be connected with namaskeak, namkeak, namkas. These meanings are derived from the New England Algonquin tongues, the accessible material of which is very meagre."

It seems, at least, as if the meaning of Witteguergaugum as here given is incorrect. There was no mill near the lake until the tannery was begun in 1871. Many pickerel are found in Big lake.

Lewis Mitchel, a member of the tribe living at Pleasant Point, and well versed in the history and traditions of his tribe, has given the following information in regard to the names of the two lakes:

"Witteguergaugum, or that country called Wittiguamuk, or Wet-gua-you-tic- Landing Place."

"Ktchinusangnagum (Big lake) meaning Big Elm Lake from the word Chesagnipk, an Elm tree."

He also gives this little sketch of Passamaquoddy demonology.

"Wenaukmees—seen by the Indians often. They make curious pictures on the rocks and sand beaches." (These pictures are said to have been a subject of investigation by the American Bureau of Ethnology.)

"Kewagh— a wanderer of the Forest. These creatures

have pieces of ice attached to their hearts. The more ice a Kewagh has the more powerful and wicked he is. They are giants. When a victim is captured he can be turned into a Kewagh."

"Chepelagh, or Atwaskemkes—creatures who have two wings, two legs but no bodies. They wander through the woods with stone hatchets with which they cut down trees with one blow."

"Mikemwess—creatures about the size of a five years old boy. They are seen by the Passamaquoddies often. The last one to visit Point Pleasant was seen by two Indians now living. The visit occurred about thirty years ago."

The story, in the words of Lewis Mitchel is as follows:

"Early in the 16th century, little after the Indians converted to Roman Catholic religion by De Monts missionaries, the Indians, after making the spring maple sugar, always camped at the foot of Grand lake stream to spear fish (land locked salmon) by torch light. One fine afternoon they heard an unearthly noise with piercing shrieks. Such noise was never, never heard by them before. They all frightened. The old men and women said, "It is Kewagh!"

The noise came toward the encampment very fast. Along toward sun down he was less than a mile to them. All the children and women and old people are placed in the canoes. The men prepared to fight. By order of some old man, or chief, all the bullets marked Cross and all the trees in front of the encampment toward the noise also marked Cross. Just after he turned back. He was bothered. Probably not less than fifty dogs they heard till midnight. Next morning they went to the swamp and saw nothing but human tracks. That the only Kewagh ever visited Passamaquoddy."

How genuine is the belief in these demons may be questioned perhaps, but it is evident that at times the old, dark, supernatural jungle of personified Indian thoughts does break through the superimposed layers of Christianity and civilization.

The first two of the following stories were told to Mr.

APPENDIX

Arthur Wheaton by Gabriel Tomah. They are here written down as well as they could be remembered after once hearing them. Gabriel Tomah always used the feminine pronoun she instead of the masculine he. "By jolly" was a favorite expression with him, and also with many Indians who used to come to Grand Lake Stream The first story is a true account of Tomah's father's attempt to reach Hudson bay.

"Father, she been told heap big water way off north west. By jolly, father, she want new hunting ground, want see country. Father and two Injuns start, take guns—canoes, go up lake, up Penobscot, up Allegash, go to northern branch St. Lawrence, go on and on into water no know, by jolly, beyond where white folks live—run into bad Injuns, but no find big water. Two Injuns heap 'fraid, turn back; but father, she go on, she no 'fraid. Go on to August. She no come to big water, she no find game, she hungry, tired, winter coming, she turn back. She go and go. It all new country. She no come this way. Bumby, father, she come to Injuns. Injuns good, give father food. She tired, she go sleep in camp. In morning, by jolly father's clothes, they all drop off! Squaw steal buttons in night; wear 'em on string round neck for ornament!

Father came 'way, she travel; she travel long time. Game all gone. Father, she most starve, clothes all rags, no buttons, all tied on! November come. Bumby, father she come to river, have no canoe. She walk 'long it. Night come. It rain, then snow, no dry wood, nothing to make fire. By jolly, father, she heap tired! She cold, clothes all rags, wind go through 'em, eugh! Rain go through, nothing to eat. Father so weak she no go more. She look 'round, see cedar tree, bark all wet, but father, by jolly, father, she strip it off—heap great strips. She put some on ground, sit on it, draw up knees, cover all over with bark, have big piece on head. She go sleep. Bumby, nine o'clock night, she hear sound chopping. It dark. She put out hand, make mark in snow in direction sound. Morning come. She see mark. Father stiff; she hardly move. She groan, try, no good. She sit on ground. Poor father! But bumby she try 'gain, get hold tree. She pull self up then. She heap cold, weak, clothes all falling off, all rags, no good nohow, nothing to eat; but father, she go slow like mark says, and bumby, by jolly, she come to lumber wagon. Four horses! Father, she look so bad man driving 'fraid! Go leave father, go back camp, tell boss. Boss know something, come out, look for father, find him, see what trouble. Boss know something. Boss take father camp; give clothes, give place to sleep, say to cook: "You burn bread little, put hot water on it, so make tea." Bumby, father, she wake up, then drink from burnt bread, feel better. Boss, she know something! Bumby give father plenty food, and by jolly, in week, father, she all right! She stay in camp all winter; she go down Miramichi river in spring with drive of logs. Then, by jolly, father, she come home! She been gone a year."

The second story is one of the mystic legends in which the tribe delight. One day Tomah was asked what makes the wind blow.

"What, white man no know that? Injun know that. It this way:"

"Cloos Crumpo, she young man. The wind blow down lake heap plenty, by jolly! Cloos Crumpo, she had 'nough of it. Bumby she say to mother, Nicitoma, "Get meat. I go way. I find wind where she live. I settle her." So Nicitoma get heap meat, and Cloos Crumpo, she put it on back. She get in canoe, she paddle up Witteguegaugum; she paddle up lakes and lakes, oh heap many lakes, until, by jolly, she come to end! She walk through woods five days, then come to heap, big high mountain. She climb up, up. On top is heap big, high stone. On top stone is heap, old man. She have white hair, white wings. She old man Makewind, and by jolly, how she make wind blow! Cloos Crumpo, she mad; she heap mad. She take old man Makewind, and throw down off stone. "By jolly," she say, "I guess we no have wind blow all time now!"

Cloos Crumpo, she come home. She happy.

Bumby, Injuns no like no wind. Flies bite; water muddy; it bad; fish no live; it hot; it smell; oh heap bad smell! lnjuns all sick. So CloosCrumpo, she go back up lakes, go through woods to heap big, high mountain. She find old man Makewind all crumpled up at foot of heap big, high stone—one wing all broken. Cloos Crumpo, she get grass and leaves; she make paste to stick. She take off hunting shirt. She stick wing together and bind with shirt. Then she put old man Makewind on heap big, high stone again. Pretty soon, bumby, wind blow; rain come; flies blow way; water get clean;—get high in lake; fish live; lnjuns get well. Everything all right! Bumby, sometimes, broken wing get tired. Then wind no blow; flies come; fish die; water muddy;lnjuns sick; heap smell; everything all bad! Then Cloos Crumpo, she go fix wing 'gain."

The following stories were told by members of the Passamaquoddy tribe to their agent, Mr. Wallace Brown. They are two of several told the writer in a short interview. In writing them down later some details were not remembered, but it is hoped a few of the inconsistences and, in each, the main plot—so far as there is one—have been preserved. Inconsistences, says Mr. Brown, are in nearly all Indian stories.

Story of the Altered Messages

One day the chief of the tribe went hunting up in the woods where Princeton now is. While he was there his wife gave birth to twins. There was much rejoicing in the tribe and the chief's father-in-law made pictures on birch bark which would tell him what had happened, and dispatched it to the father. The boy entrusted with the message stopped at a wigwam over night for the journey was long. Living in the wigwam was a girl who was in love with the chief. In he night when the boy was asleep she found the piece of bark upon which was the message, and read it. It said: "Your wife has twins, a boy and a girl." She changed it by a few marks to read. "Your wife has twins, a pig and a dog."

The next morning the boy continued his journey, and

found the chief. The latter was perturbed after he had examined the message, but he gave the boy a return message which read: "Keep them until I come back." The boy stopped at the same wigwam on the way home and the girl, again finding his message altered it to read: "Kill them before I get back."

When the father-in-law read these words he was puzzled and sad, but he said that the chief must be obeyed. Secretly, however, he killed a doe and a young deer and buried them, pretending they were his daughter and her children. Her he took far away in the woods, bound the babes to her breasts, and cut the cords of her arms. She and the children wandered about the woods for years. In the meantime the chief returned home. He was surprised and angry when they told him that his wife and her children had been killed. So his father-in-law told him what he had done. The chief and all of the tribe searched the woods for many days, but the mother and babies could not be found. The chief grew very sad. He wandered up and down in the woods a great many times. One day he was near a cave on the bank of the St. Croix where Milltown now is. Now it was in this cave that his wife had been hiding all of this time. Several years had passed. When the woman saw him she said to her children:

"Go, he is your father. He is angry with us. I do not know why, but perhaps he will be good to you."

So the children went out to meet their father, and the mother went up on top of the cave and threw herself from it to the falls in the river. The falls were strong and treacherous, and they killed her.

The chief saw the mother die. He took his children up in his arms, and asked them many questions about her. Then he took the children to the tribe.

"Be very good to them," he said.

He went back to the cave. He sprang to its top, and stood looking down into the roaring water for a long time. At length he too threw himself into the falls and was drowned.

APPENDIX

Katahdin and Red Rose

Once there was a girl who was called Red Rose. She was very beautiful. One day she wandered in the woods a long way from home. At length she came to a place from which she could see Mount Katahdin. As she looked at it she wished that she could have a husband as big and strong as the mountain. She had walked a very long way, and she was very tired. So while she thought of the husband she would like to have she sat down by the foot of a tree, and presently she fell asleep. When she awoke there was an immense Indian standing before her.

"I am the spirit of Katahdin," he said. "I know your wish. I have come to marry you."

He asked her to go to the mountain with him. It was a very long way.

"I cannot walk so far," she said.

"I did not ask you to walk," he answered. "I will carry you."

So he sat her upon his shoulder, and went away with her to Katahdin. The entrance to the mountain was in its side between some rocks where it could not be easily found. The spirit of Katahdin took her within the mountain past the rocks and there she dwelt with him most happily.

By and by a little boy and a little girl were born. As the years passed, however, Red Rose began to grow homesick.

"I wish I could go home," she said one day.

"You shall have your wish," answered the spirit of Katahdin. He gave her some medicine that made her once more young and beautiful. As a parting gift he said that whenever the girl passed her hand over her lips her words should come true, and that at whatever the boy pointed a finger should die.

So Red Rose went home to her tribe by the great waters of the Passamaquoddy bay. She took with her the little girl and the little boy. When they reached home it was a time of famine. There was nothing to eat in the wigwams;

there was no game in the woods; there were no fish in the bay nor in the river and lakes. Everybody was sad. Red Rose felt sad also, but the little girl passed her hand over her mouth and said that there was game in the woods. At once the woods were full of game. The little boy pointed his finger at a deer and it fell dead. Then he pointed at a moose and that fell dead. He happened to point at an Indian and he too fell dead. The little girl passed her hand over her mouth and said that all the lakes and rivers were full of eels. Then they were full of eels, and there was a great deal to eat. Everybody was happy, and there was no more famine.

By and by the tribe had a great fight with the Micmacks, the Indians to the east. The spirit of Katahdin came and gave to the people of Red Rose a magic bow. Arrows shot out from it in every direction, and every arrow killed an enemy. The Micmacks were frightened and fled. Katahdin also gave Red Rose more medicine so that every one hundred years she becomes young and beautiful again. Every one hundred years she comes back to visit the tribe, and she is very, very beautiful indeed.

It is said among the Indians that many present grandparents saw Red Rose when she came on the last century visit. For a long time Indians were afraid—some are still— to go up to the top of Mount Katahdin lest they meet the Spirit of the Mountain who dwells in its heart beyond the secret stone portals.*

---

*Some very interesting stories told to Mr. C. C. Leland by members of this tribe are to be found in the Century Magazine for September, 1884.

www.ingramcontent.com/pod-product-compliance
Lightning Source LLC
Chambersburg PA
CBHW022134080426
42734CB00006B/352